# Baby Boom
# BELIEVERS

*Why we think we need it all and
how to survive when we don't get it*

## MIKE BELLAH

Tyndale House Publishers, Inc.
Wheaton, Illinois

Scripture quotations are from the *New American Standard Bible.* Copyright 1960, 1962, 1963, 1971, 1973 by The Lockman Foundation.

Library of Congress Catalog Card Number 88-50459
ISBN 0-8423-0342-1
Copyright 1988 by Mike Bellah
Printed in the United States of America

3   4   5   6   7   8   9   10   95   94   93   92   91   90

# Baby Boom
## BELIEVERS

For

## CHARLOTTE

*my favorite baby boomer*

# CONTENTS

# Acknowledgments

The French philosopher Blaise Pascal said that it is presumptuous for an author to call his words "mine," since there is usually in those words much more of other people's thoughts than the author's own. That is true of this work, and I want to begin by acknowledging three authors whose thoughts have greatly influenced the pages that follow.

I discovered Landon Jones in 1982 in the footnotes of John Naisbitt's best-selling *Megatrends*. Jones' book *Great Expectations*, published in 1980, is still the most definitive book on the baby boom generation. The author's thorough research, coupled with his uncanny perception, makes this book must reading for anyone wanting to understand baby boomers. I quote Jones several times in chapters 2 and 3, but I heartily recommend reading him in full.

I first heard Charles Swindoll in Fullerton, California, in 1976, when his church was still holding five services each Sunday in the old building on Malvern Street. "Pastor Chuck's" message on Romans 7 changed my life and helped me face my self-defeating expectations for the first time. Since that time I have joined the thousands of American evangelicals who have been frequently tutored by this gifted communicator of God's Word. I have not quoted him directly in these pages, but Swindoll fans will recognize much of what I have to say, especially in chapters 5 and 6, as being influenced by Pastor Chuck.

Finally, I must acknowledge another author who died twenty-five years ago, but whose books continue to exert a major influence on the church. C. S. Lewis often championed the reading of old books. He believed we should read at least one old book for every three new ones because,

> They will not flatter us in the errors we are already committing. . . . Two heads are better than one, not because either is infallible, but because they are unlikely to go wrong in the same direction.

As I have struggled with the expectation-raising messages of the modern church, Lewis's old books have provided the challenge to bring me back to a more realistic and, I believe, biblical approach.

I am grateful also to the many friends who have helped give birth to this book. Many of them read, proofed, and made good suggestions. Others offered much needed encouragement to help me keep at it when the task seemed insurmountable. I want to thank specifically the small Bible study group in Canyon, with whom I first shared these words, and my flock at the Evangelical Fellowship in Amarillo, a group of mostly baby boomers, who continue to stimulate and encourage my study.

I am grateful to my wife, Charlotte, who is always my best critic and most loyal fan, and to my children, Janet, Jon, Josh, Joni, and Jeremy, who now know much more about the baby boom generation than they ever cared to know.

Finally, I am deeply indebted to Joy Brenneman, my excellent typist, who has survived both my illegible handwriting and my constant revisions (nearly two dozen) to bring this work to completion. Tyndale House Publishers took a chance on me when others would not. For this, and their excellent editing and marketing help, I am profoundly grateful.

# The Cinderella That Wasn't

I feel like Frank Morison, who in 1930 authored the book *Who Moved the Stone?* Morison's first chapter is called "The Book That Refused to Be Written." In it he describes how as a young skeptic he set out to destroy Christianity by disproving the historicity of Christ's resurrection. Yet his research convinced him otherwise, and his book attacking Christianity became one which supported it.

I too planned to one day write a book which would have been drastically different from the one I have written. When I became a Christian over twenty years ago, I dreamed of one day authoring a book on the "victorious Christian life." It would have set forth the keys to the instant joy, peace, and general success I had found in coming to Christ.

My testimony in those early days read much like the story of Cinderella. Before receiving Christ as my Savior and Lord, life for me had been filled with emotional turmoil, strained relationships, and general despair. But when I became a Christian "old things passed away" *quickly and totally*, and I discovered peace and happiness as I had never known. I was more successful in life. There were temporal benefits to being a Christian. I felt like Cinderella living in the palace of the prince.

I wish I could say that I lived happily ever after, but if I had, I would probably have written the other book. Instead, I've penned words about great expectations left mostly unfulfilled. I've spoken of harsh realities and human struggles, of a life that is more like a battleground than a palace.

But these are not the words of a cynic, only a realist and, I hope, a biblicist. You see, life is not a fairy tale, and Christians do not experience Cinderella-type existence. And if you think they should, such expectations will not only disappoint you, they will defeat you. There is a real peace and joy in the Christian life, but you will never discover the happiness that is until you face and discard the happiness that is not. It is my prayer that this book will help you do so.

*Mike Bellah*
Canyon, Texas

# CHAPTER 1

## *Do You Expect Too Much?*

Do you remember family vacations as a child? Do you remember getting there—the long hours in the car with brothers and sisters who kept violating your space?

Remember the endless questions for Mom and Dad? "Are we there yet? When will we get there? Can we stop now? When can we go to the bathroom?"

My dad always answered such questions by painting a rather bleak picture of our progress. "Relax," he would say. "We'll be driving all day. It's still hundreds of miles away. We'll stop again in an hour or two."

It was rarely as bad as he predicted. We always seemed to get to our destination early. We usually were pleasantly surprised when the long trip ended abruptly. And our expectations seemed to affect our attitudes in transit. We weren't overly restless and bored. Knowing we had a long trip ahead, we usually just sat back and enjoyed the ride.

When I grew up and began taking vacations with my own family, I took a different approach. My goal on the trip was to get there quickly, with a minimum number of stops. In fact, I wanted to set records. "We shaved fifteen minutes off the trip this time," I would proudly announce to my wife. (For some reason she never seemed to share my enthusiasm.)

And, in fact, we rarely did set records. As the family grew (there are now seven of us), the length of our trips grew in proportion. (I have done careful research on vacation driving time and now estimate that you should add five minutes per hour per child, plus another three minutes per hour for children under six. And for every especially strong-willed child, you multiply the whole equation by two.)

Not only did we arrive later, but, thanks to my high expectations, we arrived more frustrated, more unhappy, and less satisfied with the process.

I've learned something in recent years from my dad's example. Our expectations in life have much to do with our happiness and contentment. If they are too high, we are usually restless, frustrated, bored, unhappy, and unproductive.

I've also learned that the Bible addresses our expectations. Jesus taught His disciples not to expect too little or too much.

The disciple Philip, for instance, expected too little at the feeding of the five thousand. You may remember his response when Jesus asked how they were going to feed that crowd. "Philip answered Him, 'Two hundred denarii worth of bread is not sufficient for them, for everyone to receive a little' " (John 6:7). Andrew was a little more help, but not much more optimistic: "There is a lad here who has five barley loaves and two fish, but what are these for so many people?" (John 6:9).

Why did Philip expect too little? It was not because he pronounced the mission naturally impossible. It was. It would take a lot of Big Macs to feed that crowd, and there were no golden arches in sight.

Philip's problem was that he expected too little from *supernatural* means. Standing next to him was God in the flesh, the same God who had rained manna from heaven to feed not five thousand but 2 million Hebrews. This God could surely multiply the boy's loaves and fish!

Yes, it is wrong to expect too little, but Jesus taught with equal conviction that it is wrong to expect too much.

In Luke 14 Jesus gave instructions to the overexpecter.

> When you are invited by someone to a wedding feast, do not take the place of honor, lest someone more distinguished than you may have been invited by him, and he who invited you both shall come and say to you, "Give place to this man," and then in disgrace you proceed to occupy the last place. But when you are invited, go and recline at the last place, so that when the one who has invited you comes, he may say to you, "Friend, move up higher"; then you will have honor in the sight of all who are at the table with you (Luke 14:8-10).

What practical words! Have you ever expected recognition and then failed to receive it? Ever told your friends and family of an honor you would most likely receive, only to be humiliated and embarrassed when another got "your" award? No wonder Jesus concludes, "For everyone who exalts himself shall be humbled, and he who humbles himself shall be exalted" (Luke 14:11).

Jesus equates expecting too much with exalting oneself, something we call pride. Why? It's because the overexpecter thinks he deserves something he really doesn't. He has what one sociologist calls "a psychology of entitlement." What others consider privileges, he thinks are rights.

So Jesus warned His disciples against expecting too much. And not only against expecting too much honor, He also said not to expect too much peace (Luke 12:51-53), respect (John 15:20), authority (Mark 10:42-45), or prosperity (Luke 9:57-58).

How about you? Do you expect too much in life? The following questions have been designed to help you see if you do.

## GROUP I

Do you remember the debut of Barbie and Batman, Twiggy and Twinkies?

Have you ever worn a coonskin hat, done the twist, or used a hula-hoop?

Do you remember the names of Little Joe Cartwright's brothers, Ozzie Nelson's sons, and Rin Tin Tin's and Lassie's masters?

Can you remember a few lines from the Beatles' "All You Need Is Love," Simon and Garfunkel's "Sound of Silence," the Mamas' and the Papas' "California Dreamin' "?

Are you into nostalgia? Do you like to remember the good ol' days? Were those days much more pleasant than the ones you now experience?

## GROUP II

Do you remember your youth as a basically happy time with great expectations, expectations which have gone mostly unrealized in your adult life?

Ever feel like a victim of the times?

Do you often feel anxious and depressed?

Do you try to make up for the big things you can't have in life by indulging in little things you can?

Are you significantly committed to others? Or are you threatened by close and long-term relationships? Have you changed jobs often? How about careers?

Have you given up on your dreams? Do you no longer set goals, make resolutions?

Are you a perpetual dreamer? Do you set extremely high goals which others consider unrealistic?

Are you often discontent, restless, bored?

Do you find yourself consistently using TV, movies, vacations, or shopping trips to try to cheer you up?

Do you buy a lot on credit? Are you heavily in debt?

Do you fall easily for get-rich-quick schemes or success seminars that promise fast and easy results? Do you often enter sweepstakes or buy lottery tickets?

Have you become somewhat cynical on life? Are you tired of all the cliches and broken promises? Have you decided to expect the worst, to trust no one?

If you answered yes to many or most of the first group of these questions, I can probably guess your age. You are, like me, most likely a member of the baby boom generation born from 1946 to 1964. Simply being born and raised in this era will make you prone to overexpecting. It was a time of great expectations.

If you answered yes to many or most of the second group of these questions, you are more than just a baby boomer. You are one of the many baby boomers who are already showing signs of expecting too much. Your expectations in life are most likely both unbiblical and unrealistic. And, like my vacation expectations, they are probably self-defeating. By holding on to them you are hurting yourself.

The good news is you can do something about it. The Bible has a liberating message for the overexpecter, but first you may need some background information. You need to see how your expectations were born. You need to explore the legacy of the baby boom generation.

In the pages to follow you will meet baby boomers like Jack, Susan, Jim, and Cathy. They are people that have one thing in common: Their expectations have left them both frustrated and unproductive. They are not, however, real individuals. I have created them to help illustrate my text.

Though they are fictitious, you will recognize many if not most of these people. They could live in your city as well as mine. They could be your next door neighbor, your coworker, your friend, or your spouse. In fact, you may decide I have spent time dogging your trail. If you expect too much in life, get ready to come face to face with yourself in these pages.

# How Our Expectations Were Born: The Legacy of the Baby Boom

In May 1946, just nine months after V-J-Day, there was a record number of American births—over a quarter million babies. By the end of December, an all-time U.S. record had been set with 3.4 million births. The biggest baby boom in the history of the world had begun.

But the baby boom did not end, as one might expect, when the returning GIs had made up for lost time. It was not simply a postwar phenomenon, as Landon Jones, managing editor of *Money* magazine, observed in his book *Great Expectations: America and the Baby Boom Generation.*

> It began . . . in 1946, but instead of stopping in the 1950s (as in Europe), the tidal wave of births continued, affecting all races and classes with astonishing uniformity. This national euphoria . . . peaked in 1957, when more than 4.3 million babies were born. At least 4 million babies were born

in each of the bumper-crop years from 1954 through 1964, the last real year of the baby binge. All totaled, 76,441,000 babies—one-third of our present population—arrived in the 19 years from 1946 through 1964.[1]

Thus one sociologist has called the baby boom a nation within a nation. Another compares it to a pig in a python. As the snake swallows the pig, it moves through the length of the reptile's body, alternately stretching and collapsing each new segment of skin. The baby boom has and continues to do so with American culture.

The baby boom's influence on our society began "literally from the bottom up."[2] As infants the baby boomers helped the diaper industry revenues double by 1957. In 1953 one out of ten Americans was eating baby food at a rate of 1.5 billion cans a year—nearly a 600 percent increase from 1940.

As children, the baby boomers made Dr. Benjamin Spock both famous and wealthy. Born the same year as the first of them, Spock's *Baby and Child Care* has now sold over 30 million copies—the most widely read book in America after the Bible.

We children of the boom stimulated our society to create new schools, suburbs, coonskin hats, and Disneyland. In 1955 Fes Parker first donned the buckskins of Davy Crockett, and the wholesale price of raccoon skins went from $.26 to $8.00 a pound. Before it ended, the Crockett craze gave us over three thousand varieties of Davy's paraphernalia, everything from sweatshirts to toothbrushes. Baby boom children helped popularize the station wagon, helped McDonald's sell millions of hamburgers, and built the toy industry into a billion-dollar giant.

As teens, the baby boom's most memorable effect on society was the advent of rock music.

The baby boomers *were* the rock audience. Rock was the soundtrack in the movie version of their lives. They discovered it, danced to it, romanced to it, went to college to it, protested to it, got married to it, and someday will presumably be buried to it.[3]

Baby boomer teens also caused such overnight fads as the hula-hoop and the miniskirt. In 1958 Wham-O Corporation invented the hula-hoop, and by year's end 20,000 per day were being produced. But suddenly in 1959 the market collapsed. You couldn't give a hula-hoop away. The baby boom was demonstrating a new principle of economics that is still in effect. Our economic clout has given us the power to make and break entire industries, sometimes overnight.

As young adults, we created an unprecedented boom in higher education. We were the best-educated generation in history — twice as likely as our parents to go to college, three times as likely as our grandparents. Today over 25 percent of baby boomers have attended at least four years of college.

Not all was positive about the boom's early adulthood. It was a tumultuous time in American history. The older baby boomers gave us Woodstock, campus protests, marijuana, and a new wave of religious cults.

In mid-life we boomers became the Me Generation. We popularized jogging, health clubs, natural foods, and tanning spas. We created yuppiedom, designer clothes, a boom in psychiatric therapists, and the popular advent of the mid-life crisis.

As parents, baby boomers gave us working moms, blended families, and latchkey kids. We even changed the names of the next generation. Instead of using traditional names like Stephen, Charles, Susan, and Mary, baby boomers were and are naming their offspring such names as Brian, Jason, Nicole, and Ashley.

As the first baby boomers turned forty in 1986, the talk was of new political clout. Said Republican consultant Lee Atwater, "Any politician with one scintilla of political sense is going to go straight after the baby boom."[4]

And well they should. Baby boomers now make up about half the electorate, a statistic *Fortune* magazine says "both major parties know by heart."[5]

Thus from infancy through mid-life and, predictably, through the retirement years, the baby boom has stretched and will continue to stretch the skin of American culture. We have and will continue to be shaped by it, as Landon Jones has observed.

> No single generation has had more impact on us than the baby boom, and no single person has been untouched. The baby boom is, and will continue to be, the decisive generation in our history.[6]

What does the baby boom generation have to do with our expectations? Landon Jones has written perhaps the most definitive work on the baby boom. He entitled his book *Great Expectations* because he contends it is our great expectations, more than any other single sociological or psychological influence, that bind us baby boomers together. It is my contention that these expectations have also helped create a church of overexpecters, a situation we will examine more closely in later chapters.

How did we develop great expectations? At least five factors contributed to the baby boom's idealism.

## AFFLUENT TIMES

According to Landon Jones, our economic expectations are based not on life now, but life when we were young.[7] So what was economic life like in the early days of the baby boom? What was the economic climate that produced our expectations?

The answer is that the fifties and sixties were uniquely affluent times in American history. In the twenty-five years after World

War II our parents saw their family income double in real pur-
chasing power.

In fact, most economists believe the baby boom itself was greatly
responsible for this unparalleled national affluence. A banner
headline in *Life* printed in 1958 at the height of the boom read:
"Kids: Built-in Recession Cure — How 4,000,000 a Year Make Millions in Business."

How did these affluent times affect us?

> For most of human history, people had thought that life
> was hard, brutal, and tragic. But the baby boom's early af-
> fluence developed in it what Daniel Yankelovich has called
> "the psychology of entitlement." What other generations
> have thought *privileges*, the baby boomers thought were
> *rights*.[8]

Do you remember the discussion of overexpecters in chapter 1? Overexpecters are those who think they deserve something
they really do not. We baby boomers were raised to believe we
deserved a college education — for us and our children — whether
we could afford it or not. We deserved a secure retirement. We
deserved the best medical care. We deserved a nice home in the
suburbs. We deserved not just the pursuit of happiness. We
deserved to be happy.

Now, it is not abnormal for children to have unrealistic expectations, but those expectations are usually changed quickly and
abruptly by childhood reality. Johnny jumps out the window and
finds out he really isn't Superman. But the baby boom had no
such rude awakening in childhood. Our affluence cushioned us
from the harsh economic realities of life, and thus our unrealistic expectations went unchallenged. "All those kids at Woodstock
could afford to be there because they knew, down deep, that they
could always get jobs if they needed them."[9]

Jack and Susan were not at Woodstock, but as teens they watched it on TV. Now in their mid-thirties, they are fighting desperately to fulfill the economic dream of their youth. One key ingredient in that dream is a nice home in the suburbs. "Nothing extravagant," says Jack, "something similar to the two-story, four-bedroom Mike and Carol Brady lived in on the 'Brady Bunch' would do."

The problem is that a house similar to the Bradys' now costs well over $150,000 in most cities. And with interest rates in double digits, even Jack's and Susan's two-career income can't qualify them for a loan. "Sure we feel deprived," says Susan, "we expected steak and we're having to eat Spam. It's not easy changing your tastes."

## NATIONAL OPTIMISM

Not only were the fifties and sixties a uniquely affluent time in American history, they were also a uniquely optimistic period. Perhaps the phenomenon can best be described by comparing it with the postwar baby boom in other countries. There were only three other nations that sustained the same prolonged and broad-based baby boom as did the United States. These were Canada, Australia, and New Zealand.

Why? What trait did these countries share that made them, along with the U.S., act so differently from our European allies? Landon Jones believes it was their great expectations.

These were the countries of hope, new worlds where lives could begin again. Canada, Australia, New Zealand, and the United States were all originally settled by long-distance immigrants, people who had staked their lives on the future. All four countries, further, had both rich natural resources and a frontier open for settlement. All were spacious and were considered underpopulated. All four countries had—and *still* have—the world's highest rates of individual mobility.[10]

Countries of hope spawn optimistic attitudes in society, which in turn spawn an increased birth rate. Not only did national optimism give birth to our expectations, it gave birth to us. Jones says that our mothers ascribed to a new "procreation ethic"; having kids was seen as their patriotic duty. Perhaps this national pride in our nation's youth peaked in 1967 when *Time* magazine honored the under-twenty-five generation as Man of the Year. Wrote *Time*,

> In its lifetime, this promising generation could land on the moon, cure cancer and the common cold, lay out blight-proof, smog-free cities, help end racial prejudice, enrich the underdeveloped world and, no doubt, write an end to poverty and war.[11]

What heavy expectations to lay on one generation! Well, at least we landed on the moon. That's one down and only eight to go!

Dick remembers the national optimism and pride of the mid-sixties. It was then he enlisted in the army and went off to serve his country in Vietnam.

Now Dick is cynical. Raised on John Wayne and Audie Murphy movies, he expected a hero's welcome after his tough and much-decorated tour of duty. But like so many others, he came home to a nation that no longer believed in the war he had fought. For the Vietnam vet there were no welcoming parades, little respect, and almost no jobs.

"I feel like I was raped," says Dick. "They took my youth, my innocence, my heart and soul, and for what? The Vietnamese were abused before we came, while we were there, and after we left. Our sacrifice meant nothing."

## PARENTAL PROMISES AND PERFECT KIDS

If the expectation-raising messages sent by the affluent times and national optimism of the fifties and sixties were less than subtle, baby boom parents were probably even more blatant in conveying the message that the Good Life was something we all deserved. After all, we were clearly the center of attention.

It was a time, says Landon Jones, "when parents were making their kids their religion."[12] Their affluence would bring their children the best of everything. No amount of attention and no amount of money was too much. Everything—schools, teachers, homes, toys—had to be the best.

The kids of the baby boom would be, in the words of William Manchester,

> adorable as babies, cute as grade school pupils and striking as they entered their teens. After high school they would attend the best colleges and universities in the country, where their parents would be very, very proud of them.[13]

And proud they were. We were raised to be smarter, healthier, and more successful than any before us. We were the luckiest generation alive. That message was not lost on the baby boom. We knew we were special.

Now there is certainly nothing wrong with being raised to believe you are special. There is, however, something tragically wrong with being raised to believe you are favored. It is unrealistic to assume that since you are special, God will change the rules for you, and you can always have the seat of honor at banquets. It is wrong to think that life will keep on being hard for others, but not for you.

Jim remembers his father's promises. That's why he is a work-aholic. Jim's dad was an assembly-line worker who often put in hours of overtime so Jim would be able to go to dental school. "You're not going to just scrape by like your mother and I do." Jim can still hear his dad's words.

So Dr. Jim is a driven man trying desperately to "not just scrape by," yet wondering every day if he really is better off financially than his blue-collar father. "Sometimes it all seems so pointless," says Jim. "What good is more money when you never stop working long enough to enjoy it?"

## TELEVISIONLAND AND AN UNREAL WORLD

But parents of the baby boom did not have to raise our expectations all by themselves. They had a new built-in baby-sitter which would instruct us even more than they could. The baby boom was the first generation to be raised on TV. It was our constant companion.

> By the time an average child of the baby boom reached the age of 18, he or she would have been under television's hypnotic influence an average of 4 hours a day for 16 years. The total of roughly 24,000 hours—one-quarter of a person's waking life—is more than children spend in classrooms or with their parents.[14]

How did television raise our expectations? It did so by creating what one person called a "fun-house mirror reflection of reality." Television distorted our view of reality.

There was violence but rarely blood or pain. There was death but never emptiness. People did not work regularly but were rarely hungry or in need. In fact, economic realities were not present at all. There was little unemployment in Televisionland and no food stamps. Fathers were not wage-earners but hapless buffoons, outwitted by both their children and their wives. There was desire in Televisionland, but lust and greed were somehow mixed up with craving for prettier hair and whiter laundry. Actions have no consequences in Televisionland. When everything is subject to change or cancellation, life becomes absurd.[15]

Not only was life absurd on TV, it was unrealistic. One writer described the idealism of television in the fifties and sixties in this way:

No one is ever alone in Televisionland. There is little real despair. Problems can be worked out and almost always are. More TV parents are widowed than divorced. Anger is cute, rarely ugly. A child who would believe television would believe that most problems are solvable, usually within the half hour, and that sacrifices and compromises rarely involve human pain.[16]

Beaver Cleaver never had a parent die from cancer or suffer a nervous breakdown or leave home to live with Eddie Haskel's mom. The show was entertaining. It did not, however, prepare us for reality. In fact, there was a seemingly benevolent conspiracy in the works—television worked to shield us from reality, and so did parents, teachers, and most other adults. Most adults we knew could remember the Depression and World War II. They knew about bad times, but they seemed determined that we would never feel such pain in our own lives. Because of this benevolent conspiracy, we were hardly prepared for that inevitable crisis, adolescence. Some baby boomers still haven't gotten over the shock of living in a world unlike the Televisionland of the late fifties and the sixties.

Cathy is a mother of two preschoolers. She is also deeply depressed. Even with six children the Bradys' house never looked as messy as her own. Wally and Beaver never fought with each other the way her kids do.

Why can't her husband help around home the way Ozzie Nelson helped Harriet? Why can't she look and sound as composed as June Cleaver?

"I expected raising a family to be fun and rewarding," says Cathy. "Well, so far it's just been hard and demanding."

## COMMERCIALS AND NARCISSISM

Television programs raised our expectations by idealistic drama — drama which, while unrealistic, usually contained at least a good moral lesson. The good guys fought for justice on "Bonanza." Opie Taylor learned to tell the truth on "The Andy Griffith Show."

Television commercials, however, were not nearly so altruistic. Parents and teachers may have worried about narcissism (though, unwittingly, they may have helped to produce it), but not the advertisers. They thrived on the narcissism. In fact, they built an empire on it.

By age twenty-one the average baby boomer had been bombarded by over 300,000 commercial messages, and they all carried basically the same assumption: Personal gratification is the dominant goal in life.

"You deserve a break today," counseled McDonald's. "Have it your way," added Burger King. "This I do for me," chimed in Miss Clairol. "Yes, you can have it all," echoed Michelob Light.

Is it any wonder we have become the Me Generation? We have

been told over and over again that the world revolves around us. Is it any wonder that we expect too much?

Fran is a successful executive with a public relations firm. At thirty-eight she is still single, but not by choice. "I always wanted to meet the right man and get married," she says, "but during my twenties and early thirties my career demanded all of my attention. If you want to succeed in this business, you have to be willing to sacrifice."

"But now," continues Fran, "my career goals are realized. I can settle down, get married, maybe even have a child. Only one problem—all the good men are taken, or gay, or intimidated by my success." Fran feels like she has been deceived. "I guess the commercials were wrong. You really can't have it all."

## CHRISTIAN EXPECTATIONS

In Romans 12 Paul urges us to not be "conformed to the world." But church history will show that this particular command has not been kept with great consistency. Rather than speaking God's unchanging truth into our culture, we have often had the culture shape us. The tendency has been to bend our theology (and our expectations) to fit the times. The twentieth century will undoubtedly record such a distortion.

The expectations of baby boom believers in our spiritual infancy mostly mirrored those of our secular counterparts. Those of us who came to Christ in the sixties and seventies were motivated basically by promises of personal happiness and peace, even prosperity. We were told that Jesus could make us higher than we had ever been before. And in the process He could make us more successful, more healthy, and more popular.

What television was to the secular boomer, Christian books were to the believer. The testimonies read like the story of Cinderella.

Before Christ, everything was dreadful. There even seemed to be rivalries among some writers to see who had had the most dreadful pre-conversion life. But when our hero or heroine came to Christ, they went to live in the palace and, of course, lived happily ever after.

The author did conscientiously warn that Christ never promised us a rose garden, but the smell of roses in his or her successful smile convinced us otherwise.

And if we were saved, but didn't have "victory," there was always the Christian version of the success seminar. There we could learn the "Christian's secret of a happy life" and maybe still get in the palace. All we needed to do was (pick one) "let go and let God," "pray to receive the Holy Spirit," "receive the gift of tongues," "be filled with the Spirit," "practice the power of positive thinking," "move ahead with possibility thinking," "plant some seed faith," "practice the presence of God," "name it and claim it," "learn to sit, walk and stand," or "discover the eight areas of basic youth conflict."

And while our secular counterparts dreamed of smog-free cities and cures for cancer, we dreamed of the Rapture, the event near the end of this age when Jesus will come for His own (see 1 Thessalonians 4:13-18). In the late sixties and early seventies Hal Lindsey's *Late Great Planet Earth* was the guide for baby boom eschatology. It was to the baby boom believer what Spock's book was to the secular boomer, selling millions of copies. We were premillenial and pretribulational, and expected to go any day. We believed that Christ would come back before the age of great peace and before the time of the Tribulation, and we could now be living in that very day.

Now Lindsey certainly was not a pseudo-prophet. He never set a specific date for Christ's return, and his motive was obviously to get us to live every day as if it might be our last. The problem was that we never expected to have to live every day *until* the last. We expected to escape any prolonged future tribulation. We may have expected tough days, but certainly not very many of them. *Endurance* was not something we thought would be necessary.

Tom and Kay met in the late sixties through a Christian ministry on their college campus. They were both new Christians, and their relationship grew along with their faith, and they were soon married.

Fifteen years later they are both disillusioned with Christianity. They left the church after the death of their only child, Sherry. At six, Sherry was the delight of Tom and Kay's life. Then a tragic car wreck left her in a coma.

Kay never gave up hope for Sherry's recovery. In fact, Kay's faith was the pride of her church, which "still believed in miracles" and taught that if you had enough faith "nothing would be impossible." Everyone agreed that Kay certainly had faith, and everyone in the church expected Sherry to miraculously recover.

She did not. Sherry died six months after the accident without regaining consciousness. Tom and Kay are bitter and resentful. Says Tom, "God let us down. It's that simple. We kept our part of the bargain. He did not."

Thus for the most part Christian expectations for baby boom believers have not varied significantly from our friends in the world. We, like they, expected life not to be brutal, hard, and tragic — at least not for long. And we, like they, developed a psychology of entitlement. The only difference was they thought life owed them personal happiness. We thought God did.

At any rate, the end result was that baby boom believers, like baby boomers at large, were in for an expectation bust.

# CHAPTER

## The Expectation Bust:
## When Reality Says
## You Can't Have It All

Older baby boomers can tell you exactly where they were on that fateful afternoon, November 22, 1963, when John F. Kennedy was assassinated in Dallas.

We can remember because it was the first major trauma we suffered as a group. There would be others—Vietnam, Kent State, Watergate—but this was the first and the one we felt most deeply. It was the beginning of our expectation bust.

But what troubled baby boomers most would come later in the seventies and eighties, and not on a national level, but on a personal one. It was then our personal dreams began to die.

Dr. Arthur Anderson, sociologist at Fairfield University, speaking in 1983 when U.S. colleges were still populated almost entirely by baby boomers, stated that

the problem for young people is the old American dream. College students have great anxieties about whether they will live as well as their parents lived. The old pattern of expectation—that you probably will do better than your parents—is gone. It doesn't work that way anymore.[1]

31

Our anxiety seems well-founded. Education was going to help us make it, remember? But education has not fulfilled our expectations.

Thirty years ago the lifetime earnings of the college graduate were double that of high school graduates. Now the incremental earnings for college graduates are only about 20 percent more than high school graduates. In pure economic terms, college no longer makes sense for most people.[2]

Dr. Anderson says the U.S. probably has 30,000 to 40,000 surplus Ph.D.s. "We are graduating twice as many lawyers as the country can possibly use. Half of them will never practice."[3]

Even the celebrated Harvard MBAs are in trouble. In 1983 starting salaries for these cream-of-the-crop professionals were down 6 percent from 1982 and expected to drop further.

Thus the House Select Committee on Population reported: "The baby boom generation may never achieve the relative economic success of the generations preceding it or following it."[4]

Richard Easterlin, an economist at the University of Southern California, concurs: "The present large generation will remain relatively deprived."[5]

*Money* magazine reported in March 1983 that there were twice as many competitors for every managerial opening as there were in 1975. And growing labor surpluses normally hold down salaries. The real median income of men age 25 to 34 fell 16 percent between 1973 and 1980.[6] In 1986, 35 percent of the baby boom's men and 63 percent of its women made less than $10,000 a year.[7]

To keep up with their parents' economic achievements, both baby boom parents have had to go to work. Thus 70 percent of baby boom mothers are now employed outside of the home.

The baby boom's greatest asset, its size, has become its greatest liability. Its size has caused it to face the real possibility of becoming the first generation in American history that may not expect to equal the living standards of its parents.

But jobs and salary expectations are not the only dreams baby boomers have failed to achieve. Dreams of ideal marriages have also been shattered. Fifty-two percent of all baby boomers are now divorced by age 34. This is five times the rate of our parents at the same age.[8]

Ten percent of the boom's women have remained single – not all by choice. Because of unique baby boom demographics there is, in the words of one writer, *A Great American Man Shortage*.[9] Thus some baby boom women that would have found suitable mates in another era will not in this generation.

In fact the expectation bust among baby boomers has been especially hard on its women. Raised on Barbie dolls and romance novels, boom women were not prepared for the real challenges of marriage and family. Lee Ezell, a counselor to many such women, writes of her experience:

> The more I listened, the more I heard the same familiar tale. Cinderella was forever "*waiting* for the glass slipper." Sleeping Beauty was forever *waiting* for the right kiss. And somehow, the forever-after never came. We had all believed the pretty stories, and we had all been disappointed![10]

The problem was not limited to those who had hoped for a satisfying life in the traditional role of wife and mother either. Born in 1963 with Betty Friedan's book, *The Feminine Mystique*, the modern women's movement hoped to free society from these "stifling" stereotypes. And fueled by the large number of baby boom women who joined its ranks, the movement has had many successes.

But are feminists in the late eighties satisfied? Authors Ronald and Beverly Allen don't think so.

Twenty-two years have passed since Betty Friedan wrote *The Feminine Mystique*. There are now young women and men who have grown up with the ideals of feminism and the "holy quest" for a sex-role revolution. These women have known only panty hose, not confining corsets. But now new forces are at work. Old-line feminists are expressing fatigue. Many who marched and fought for equality are now wondering where they are and why they have come. Women who have sacrificed home and family for career and fulfillment are wondering if the sacrifice was worth the reward, if the gain was worth the cost.[11]

Not only are baby boom women in trouble, the expectation bust has affected even the most cherished symbol of the great American dream, home ownership. The median price of a new house almost quadrupled from $18,000 in 1963 to $64,000 in 1980.

Family income, at the same time, trailed far behind, making the dream of home ownership even more difficult for young families. In 1970, according to an estimate by the Department of Housing and Urban Development, half of the people in the country could afford to buy the median-priced new house. Today only 13 percent can. In fact, nearly two-thirds of all American families in 1980 could not afford to purchase the homes in which they live.[12]

In 1985, first-time home buyers (80 percent of whom were baby boomers) paid a median price of $65,000 for a little under 1300 square feet of house.[13] Two years later, in the spring of 1987, interest rates fell to a nine-year low, but, at the same time, the median price of a new home topped $100,000. More baby boomers could now afford housing, but not nearly the house of their dreams.

And the baby boom's future looks even more bleak. Ronald

J. Vogel, economist at the University of Arizona, says that people age 65 and older will increase by 120 percent between the years 1980 and 2030, while the general population will grow by only 35 percent during the same time.

> More disturbing is that the over-75 population—those most in need of long-term and expensive health care—will grow at an even more rapid rate.
>
> Mix into all this medical technology that is keeping people alive longer, and the disintegration of the family, and there is a possibility of a significantly lower quality of life for the elderly of the future.
>
> There are likely to be fewer medical services, more chronic illness, and even economic "warfare" between the generations—serious enough to possibly destabilize the country.[14]

Thus, George F. Will, writing in *Newsweek* in February 1986, answers the question raised by Michelob's ad for light beer, "Who says you can't have it all?" "Sadly, the answer is: reality, that's who," says Will.[15] And so it has.

What have been the effects of the expectation bust on baby boomers? There are many, and they are as varied as they are tragic.

## VICTIMIZATION
According to psychiatrist, Robert Coles,

> We model ourselves desperately after other people because we haven't really been taught to accept the limitations of life—not when advertising offers us the moon and when one or two of us actually gets there, whereupon we conclude that in no time at all the rest of us will be following suit.

It is a grandiosity that serves the interests of those who have things to sell.[16]

And selling to the baby boom has always been big business. One result of this generation's expectation bust has been its victimization by those who hope to capitalize on our disillusionment. Who are these victimizers?

Many baby boomers, especially the youngest ones, found it difficult to live in an ambiguous world devoid of meaning and purpose. They craved the certainty that their parents, schools, and religions had been unable to give them. So they joined cults.[17]

Since the late sixties an estimated 3 million people have been involved with groups like the Moonies, Church of God, Scientology, Hare Krishna, and Synanon. The great majority of cult recruits have been disillusioned baby boomers.

But cults are not the only ones to victimize baby boomers. We have been especially susceptible to fraudulent pyramiding sales schemes. Baby boomers are prime targets for slick entrepreneurs who promise a quick and easy road to the dreams which have eluded us.

Similarly baby boomers are easy prey for loan sharks peddling easy credit at astronomical rates. Sixty-nine percent of us have consumer loans, yet less than one-third of us save money.[18] If we can't afford our dreams, we will borrow them and pay it back *mañana!*

Baby boomers enter sweepstakes and lotteries. We attend expensive success seminars. We invest in get-rich-quick schemes. We even follow success-oriented religious gurus who promise us financial success if we will only plant a little seed faith in their own hip pockets.

Gary knows what it feels like to be victimized. Five years ago

Gary, now forty, and his wife, Sue, joined the TV ministry of Pastor Bob.

Sue, who had struggled with chronic back pain, was healed by Pastor Bob in one of his famous city-wide crusades. At her urging Gary attended the meetings too and received the gift of healing himself. At least Pastor Bob told him he had felt some of his own "anointing" leave and saw it come to rest on Gary.

At Sue and Pastor Bob's urging Gary sold his recently inherited farm land and laid the proceeds at the feet of this new apostle. Pastor Bob promised him a "hundredfold" return both in money and in spiritual blessing on Gary's own healing ministry.

A few weeks later Pastor Bob left for two weeks of spiritual refreshing in the Bahamas. Gary was placed in charge of the ministry in his absence, but Pastor Bob took Sue along to "take dictation" on a new book he was writing.

Two years later Gary was fired as Pastor Bob's administrator because of what Pastor Bob called a "root of bitterness" in his spirit. Gary lost not only his inheritance and his job. He lost Sue because, as she put it, "God told me to leave father, mother, and husband and follow Him and Pastor Bob."

## DESPAIR

The Book of Proverbs says, "Hope deferred makes the heart sick," and the shattered dreams of the baby boom have done exactly that, as Landon Jones observes.

> Approaching mid-life, baby boomers are floundering. They have rejected the value system of their parents, but have come up with nothing better to replace it. All they know is that life has failed to fulfill the great expectations they had established for themselves during the fifties and sixties. . . . Psychiatrists now estimate that up to one-third of the

people in their twenties and thirties are "very depressed and anxious" most of the time.[19]

Most of the baby boomers cited thus far suffer significantly from depression. Frustrated home owners Jack and Susan do. So does Dick, the Vietnam vet. Ditto for Cathy the young mother, Jim the workaholic, and Fran the successful but husbandless executive.

For many the despair has been too great. They have opted to end their lives themselves.

Phyllis attempted suicide after her recent divorce. So did John after a depression in the oil industry forced his Texas real estate business into bankruptcy. For Jean it was her sense of failure as a mother. All three represent an eerie trend among baby boomers.

If homicide provides an accurate index of the overall crime level in society, then suicide is a similarly grim measure of social despair. And the baby boomers, especially young baby boomers, have been taking their own lives more frequently than any generation in history. In the past two decades, suicide among teenagers has tripled. It is now the leading killer of young Americans after accidents. This would not be such a startling figure if the increase were matched in other age groups, suggesting that outside social forces, perhaps inflation or unemployment, might have affected everyone equally adversely. But the astonishing fact is *that the nation's overall suicide rate has remained level over the same period.*[20]

Thus *The Big Chill,* a movie about a baby boom reunion, surprised no one by beginning with a funeral for a baby boomer who committed suicide in mid-life. Most of us know friends or family who have attempted or committed suicide. Some of us have entertained such thoughts ourselves. Dr. Carol Nadelson of the American Psychiatric Association comments on the roots of this.

In 1966, when these baby boomers were 20, there were about 16,800 psychiatrists in America. Now, there are more than twice that number—plus thousands more psychologists and psychiatric social workers. . . . These people were told promises can be fulfilled if they worked hard. But they worked hard, and their promises weren't fulfilled.[21]

And the trend toward depression and suicide shows no signs of letting up as the baby boom ages. According to psychiatrist Dan G. Blazer: "Suicide rates for the elderly can be expected to increase as the baby boom generation enters later life."[22]

## NARCISSISM

What about the baby boomers who did not take their lives? How have the living handled their depression? How have they handled the expectation bust? George Will says we handled it with compensatory consumption.

This is the saddest story ever told. A whole generation believed the Michelob beer commercial and, consequently, got its heart broken. Many baby boomers expected a pot of gold but have settled for a Dove Bar. . . . A *Wall Street Journal* report on "strapped yuppies" quotes one such: "We can't afford houses and cars, but we'll spend $2 on a Dove Bar so we can try to tell ourselves we aren't doing as badly as our pocketbooks say we are." A Dove Bar is ice cream. It is a flimsy prop for self-esteem. Many baby boomers are big spenders, but often their foreign travel, pricey audio systems, and gourmet mustards are compensatory consumption.[23]

Compensatory consumption has always been around, but it became more widespread when the baby boomers in the seventies began finding their dreams in their own pleasures. It was then that Tom Wolfe labeled us the Me Generation.

> Instead of improving society, the baby boomers were improving themselves. They were jogging, climbing mountains, painting, and playing racquetball. Faces that once sweated on picket lines were now sweating in health spas. They were concerned about the inner person, too. They were reading books with titles like *I'm OK—You're OK, Looking Out for No. 1, Power!* and *How to Be Your Own Best Friend.*[24]

According to Landon Jones, the most relevant question of the seventies was "Am I happy?" and if you were not, "You changed (pick one) your job, your spouse, your city, or your clothes."[25]

Nowhere has the baby boom's self-love been more evident than in its most celebrated subculture—the 4 million boomers (only 5 percent of the total) who actually did make it, the Yuppies.

*Newsweek* called 1984 the Year of the Yuppie, *yuppie* standing for "young urban professional" or "young upwardly mobile." Yuppies make an average of $40,000 per year. They are three times as likely as other Americans to have an American Express card, and twice as likely to engage in regular physical fitness routines.

However what unites yuppies most is what *Newsweek* calls a new state of consciousness, "Transcendental Acquisition."[26] They "live to buy." The Michelob ad "You can have it all" is their battle cry.

What do yuppies buy? *U.S. News* says that yuppies have expensive tastes.

> The name of the game is best. Buying it, owning it, using it, eating it, wearing it, growing it, cooking it, driving it, doing whatever with it.

Yuppies are said to have insatiable appetites for designer clothes, computers, video recorders, pasta makers, phone-answering devices, expresso machines, pagers and other gadgets. Volvos and BMWs are very popular. An Atlanta auto dealer reports that young adults fill a waiting list of up to 60 days for $32,500 Jaguars.[27]

But even the elite baby boomers — "so small you could fit them four to a car in all the BMWs in America"[28] — are not happy.

According to psychiatrist Douglas La Bier, the life of a yuppie often takes a psychic toll.

> A lot of them, including many with fast-track, hi-tech careers, report feelings of dissatisfaction, anxiety, depression, emptiness, paranoia, as well as a whole range of physical complaints — headaches, backaches, stomach problems, insomnia, eating problems.[29]

With their high salary expectations and willingness to work hard to get there, it is not uncommon for yuppies to work sixty-hour weeks. They thus fall easy prey to unscrupulous employers who work them at a pace they cannot sustain for long. Yuppies have an unusually high rate of professional burnout. "You can stay on the fast track for only so long even in $125 jogging shoes."[30]

And with the stock market crash of October 1987, yuppies now have a new problem. According to *USA Today* columnist Jim Meyers, they have become the scapegoats for the economic woes brought on by the "bear" market. "Suddenly all the world loves to hate yuppies. Even yuppies hate yuppies."[31]

Meyers says that yuppie greed is believed by many to have caused the crash "as well as closed the hometown factory, killed the family farm, ran up the trade deficit, and bloated the national debt."[32] Thus an article in the *Wall Street Journal* claims that Madison Avenue has now dumped the yuppies.

> They're young and they're greedy. He wears a Rolex President watch with his Brooks Brothers suspenders. She, in her power suit and floppy bow tie, carries a Coach Metropolitan bag. We—even those of us who may be a bit yuppie ourselves—hate their guts. They have too much money and spend it too freely—on themselves. Yuppies have become a bore and, under the circumstances, something of an embarrassment. Thus Madison Avenue is trying to wipe them out.[33]

How has all this negative press affected yuppies? According to Ned Hallowell of the Harvard Medical School, "They say they have no friends—no sense of gratification. They say they're blamed for everything—from air pollution to nuclear war. They hunger to belong—to a group, to a family, to something, but they don't know what."[34] And that leads us to the next result of the baby boom's expectation bust.

## ISOLATION

Not only has the baby boom's narcissism taken a psychic toll, it has taken a relational toll as well.

Do you remember Narcissus of Greek mythology? He was a strikingly handsome young man, the heart-throb of all the eligible bachelorettes of his day. Yet Narcissus could not take a lover. He already had one—a viciously jealous lover who would allow him no others.

While gazing at his own reflection in a quiet pond one day, Narcissus fell in love with himself. And his self-love consumed him. He had no room for others. Such is the fate of all who follow in his steps. Such has been the fate of the baby boom. Our narcissism has isolated us from others.

The first real casualty of the baby boom's isolation from others was the institution of marriage. Life was too short to stay in a bad marriage. If you could get instant gratification by changing TV channels, then why not marriage partners?

Mark, a recent graduate of medical school, divorced his wife of ten years because "she no longer fits my new circle of friends." Similarly, Jane left her husband after an affair with her boss because "I don't love him anymore. I love someone else." Tom and Becky decided to split up "because we always fight and life is too short to be angry all the time."

In the seventies, as baby boomers began to marry, the national divorce rate doubled. By the end of the first decade of baby boom marriages, it had tripled. Today over half of us are divorced. And if we should remarry, chances of that marriage surviving are worse than for the first.

But baby boomers have not only isolated themselves from their spouses; their children have suffered a similar fate. Says sociologist James Coleman,

> Child rearing is one of the biggest casualties of the modern age that is being ushered in by this generation. . . . We are becoming the first species in the history of the world which is unable to care for its young.[35]

Landon Jones concurs:

> No one knows anymore who is responsible for the children. A society that has to ask parents, "Did You Hug Your Child Today?" or "It's ten o'clock. Do you know where your children are?" is not expressing full confidence in parents.[36]

Jones also notes that "the cult of the child has become the cult of the adult," and the children whose parents made them their religion are making their own children their victims.[37] *Time* comments,

> The disturbing by-product of the baby boomers' quest for personal freedom, for what the "human potential" gurus call self-realization, has been lack of commitment to others. In the 1979 movie *Kramer vs. Kramer,* Meryl Streep, playing the mother who wants to see more in life than a diaper rash, writes her young son, "I have gone away because I must find something interesting to do for myself in the world. Everybody has to and so do I. Being your Mommy was one thing, but there are other things too." The fact that she comes back later to try to reclaim her son only makes the movie a more wrenching testimonial to the conflicts that racked the Boom generation as it coped with adulthood in the seventies.[38]

What affect has all this had on the children of baby boomers?

> Many of these children are emotionally and psychologically wounded. A decade earlier, the psychiatric field of childhood depression did not exist. Now it is a growth industry. Children as young as six and seven are trying to kill themselves in numbers previously unthinkable. Yet these are the same people who will carry us through the twenty-first century. Three out of every four children born in 1980 can expect to live to the year 2045; one-half will reach 2055, and one out of every four will reach 2065. They will be the real legacy of the boom generation.[39]

Nicole is not a baby boomer, but her mother is. Nicole has never met her real father, but she has observed more than half a dozen "friends" of her mom who have lived at her house for brief periods of time.

A latchkey kid, Nicole comes home most days to an empty house. She often fixes her own breakfast and supper. Not only will she probably suffer from childhood depression, Nicole has a better than normal chance of being sexually abused, becoming a runaway, and/or getting hooked on drugs.

## REGRESSION

Why does Bob Dylan still draw a crowd? Why do my kids know so much about my era when I knew so little about my parents' times? Why do we still sing the songs of the sixties?

Because the baby boom is into nostalgia—a phenomenon one writer calls a "functional emotion" for baby boomers.

> Nostalgia, then, is a functional emotion which, by shoring up a sagging sense of identity, can help either a person or a generation cope with difficult times. In nostalgia, the baby boomers have found a haven from anxiety and a means of reaffirming stable identities badly shaken during the passage from adolescence. It bears the same relationship to anxiety that aspirin does to a headache; it offers temporary relief. For the baby boomers, it was not that the past was so wonderful, it was that the present is so troubling.[40]

It is interesting to note that the nostalgia that baby boomers enjoy reflects the high school days of their older brothers and sisters and not themselves. The "Happy Days" kids like Richie and the Fonz attended high school in the late fifties and early sixties, years when the older baby boomers were still in junior high or elementary school.

There are two reasons for this. One, some of the people we

remember so fondly were our adolescent idols from an era when we still had heroes. They were the people we hoped to become. And two, this was the era before John Kennedy was assassinated. It was pre-assassination, pre-Vietnam. It was a time when we still felt secure, when our idealistic dreams were still intact.

So nostalgia helps us cope with tough times. It is therapeutic. It can be a good thing to *dream* of the past. The problem comes when we try to *live* in the past.

Psychologists call this emotional disturbance *regression*. Dr. Dan Kiley, writing in 1983, called it the *Peter Pan Syndrome*.[41] In the sixties, yippie leader Jerry Rubin yelled, "We ain't never, never gonna grow up. We're gonna be adolescents forever!" Oddly enough, Rubin did grow up. He is now a successful securities analyst on Wall Street. But some baby boomers seem to have taken his advice. Like the fictitious Peter Pan, they are refusing to grow up.

Do you know any Peter Pan-like adults? For instance, do you know any baby boom married men who are about as responsible as junior highers—who treat their wives like they once treated their mothers—who seem to always be out for too long with the gang and, as a result, are always in the doghouse?

Do you know any mid-life single or divorced women who still are naively flirtatious—who can't understand why they keep attracting the wrong kind of men?

Do you know any mid-lifers living in a perpetual state of now, where tomorrow never comes? Do you know anyone up to their ears in debt, but still buying on credit the latest cars, boats, clothes, and gadgets they just can't do without?

Do you know any single baby boom men who avoid long-term commitments at all costs—who change jobs and girlfriends as quickly as they change apartments?

Do any of these symptoms describe you? Do you sometimes try to live in the past? Peter Pan still lives, doesn't he?

Stan is a Peter Pan. As Stan approaches the free throw line, he thinks back twenty years ago to the big game with Central High. He was shooting one and one then, too. That time he missed and East High lost. Well, maybe this time he will sink them both for old times' sake.

Stan, at forty, is a Peter Pan of sports. Every weeknight will find him in the gym, on the baseball diamond, or on the soccer field. Every noon he works out at the fitness center.

Like the seven-year-old who sucks his thumb, Stan has returned to the practice of a happier time in life. For him the excitement of the game dulls the pain of a frustrated career and vanishing youth.

## UNDEREXPECTING

Perhaps the greatest irony of all is that most overexpecters ultimately end up as underexpecters.

> The short of it is that the baby boomers encountered a disastrously large gap between their aspirations and their opportunities. They had set for themselves idealistic goals that their own size made self-defeating. Worse, their failure to meet their aspirations—and the sinking realization that they might never achieve what they had set out to do—had the effect of discouraging their willingness to try. The generation wound up with a classic anxiety syndrome: high aspirations, low motivation. They were still dreamers, but were unable to take the risks necessary to achieve their dreams.[42]

Jean, a housewife and mother of preschoolers, underexpects. Frustrated because her home can't look perfect, she has lapsed into a chronic depression. Most of her days are spent staring blandly at the TV while kids scream and dishes and laundry pile higher and higher.

Carl is a real estate salesman whose early success led him to believe the real estate market would always boom. It did not. Now frustrated by spiraling interest rates and a depressed market, Carl is an underexpecter. He no longer makes an effort to sell. His days are spent sitting in his office waiting for his phone to ring or having coffee with other underexpecting sales people whose lack of enthusiasm is contagious.

Herein lies the problem with the great volume of books written to today's underexpecter. Whether you are underexpecting regarding your physical, moral, vocational, familial, or spiritual productivity, most baby boomers who have given up and quit trying are not really underexpecters. They are overexpecters in underexpecter's clothing. The symptoms are the same. The disease is not. To raise their expectations again to unrealistic heights is like giving the wrong medicine. It may harm the patient. It will certainly not help him.

And many of today's baby boomers are no longer even listening to the utopian promises of the overexpecting gurus. These baby boomers have become cynical. The cynic does not just believe that he has no solutions for his problems. Rather, he believes there are no solutions at all—not for him or for others, not for now or ever. Tom and Kay, the couple who lost their six-year-old to death, are examples of baby boom cynics. The failure of the success gospel they had embraced has not only left them discouraged, it has left them disillusioned and cynical. They are no longer receptive to the true gospel. They are convinced that there are no real answers.

## DISCONTENT

There is one more negative result of the baby boom's expectation bust, but you will probably not read of it in the secular press. It has to do with the concept of contentment.

The Bible admonishes Christians to be content. The word means to be satisfied with the normal provisions of life. (See 1 Timothy 6:6-8.) To be content is to harmonize your expectations with your reality—not to have all you want, but to want only what you have.

Baby boomers are not very content. Because our expectations are so much higher than our reality, we tend to be discontent, restless, and bored.

One result of this restlessness is a propensity for escapist activities. These activities can be fairly innocuous—TV, movies, vacations, or dining out. Or they can be quite sinful and destructive—mind-altering drugs, excessive spending, and illicit sexual activities.

Frank is a pornaholic. For him sexual fantasy is a drug. It lifts him out of the painful reality of his unrealized expectations and eases his emotional pain. It is also addicting. It demands more and more of his time and energy and hurts his relationship with God and others.

Meg is a compulsive shopper. Buying things is the drug which drowns her unfulfilled expectations. Her addiction has caused her to misuse credit, and she is heavily in debt. The problem is beginning to threaten her marriage.

## DISILLUSIONED PARENTS

Like their children, parents of baby boomers also experienced an expectation bust. They too have been subject to the same harsh economic realities of the seventies and eighties. They too have been bombarded by the same expectation-raising commercials. They too expected a brighter future.

Yet their greatest disappointment has come from a source where they least expected it—their children. In 1976 columnist Ann Landers polled her millions of readers with the question, "If you

had it to do over again, would you have children?" A full 70 percent of those responding, mostly mothers of baby boomers, said
no, they would not.

In light of the trends noted in this chapter, their answer is under-
standable. Parents of baby boomers gave to their children as no
generation of parents in the history of this nation. And what did
they get for their effort? In many cases they got depressed, self-
centered, uncommitted, immature, underachieving, and discon-
tented children. No wonder they too are disillusioned.

Ted and Marge are such parents. Their daughter, Susan, after
two unsuccessful marriages has moved back into her old room.
She brings with her two young and very ill-behaved children.

Susan often leaves the children with Marge, not only when the
day-care center at work won't take them, but, frequently, during
the evening. "I've got a right to a social life," explains Susan.

Ted and Marge are angry. "We've paid our dues," says Ted. "We've
raised our children and should not have to do so again." "But what
can we do?" continues Marge. "She is our daughter and they are
our grandchildren."

## EXPECTATION BUST IN THE CHURCH

Have Christian baby boomers undergone an expectation bust?
Do we fall prey to religious victimizers? Are we often given to despair? Are we self-centered? Do we then sometimes flee from commitment to others? Do we have any Peter Pans in the pew? Do
we underexpect? Have some of us given up? Do we struggle with
discontent, restlessness, boredom? Are parents of Christian baby
boomers sometimes disillusioned? Or does our commitment to
Christ save us from the letdown experienced by secular baby
boomers?

Speaking for both myself and my peers in the church, I have
to say that we struggle with the same expectation bust experienced

by our friends in the world. In fact, our expectation bust may have been worse for two reasons.

One, our expectations were often higher than those of non-Christian boomers. Not only did we expect what they did materially from the world; we also expected instant and complete moral changes in our character. We expected Cinderella-type testimonies, but instead we have seen the struggle with our own nature continue.

And that leads to the second reason. The results of the expectation bust (like narcissism, isolationism, regression, underexpecting) are not only tragedies for us. They are also sins. Thus we have failed twice, and our guilt is great.

But the good news for us is our expectations do not have to defeat us. Jesus taught us differently. We can survive the expectation bust, but first we will need to change the way we think.

# CHAPTER
# 4

# The Renewing of Our Minds:
# The Groundwork for
# Changing Our Expectations

We baby boomers are our own worst enemies. It is not our times but our expectations that have defeated us. But when I suggest lowering them, which is most often what I do suggest, I get strong negative reactions from religious overexpecters like Richard.

Richard is a proponent of the success gospel. He believes you can never overexpect from a God who owns the cattle on a thousand hills. His words to me are filled with emotion born of deep conviction.

"You're conforming to the world," argues Richard. "You're not believing God. 'O ye of little faith.' "

"OK, Richard, maybe you're right," I reply. "Tell me, what is faith? Is it trust? Reliance?"

"Yes," says Richard, "it's both of those."

"Trust in whom, Richard, or what?"

"God, of course," replies Richard.

"Any god?" I ask.

"No," returns Richard, "biblical faith is trust in the true and living God."

"OK," I say, "and what do I believe about this God. Is He holy and loving? How about detached and limited?"

"Yes and no," replies Richard. "He is holy. He is not limited."

"Who decides, Richard? Can I envision God anyway I please?"

"No, you must believe in Him as He really is."

"And who decides what He really is, Richard? Do you? Do I? What about Romans 10:17? 'So faith comes from hearing, and hearing by the word of Christ.' Would you agree, Richard, that the Bible defines God for us? It tells us what we should believe about Him."

"I guess so. What are you getting at?"

"Simply this, Richard. The Bible not only defines God's character. It defines His actions. Not only should my concept of God come from the Bible, my expectations from God must also be biblical."

My conversation with Richard introduces the theme of this chapter. How do I know if my expectations are good or bad? How do I know if I am expecting too much or too little? How do I know whether I'm believing God or conforming to the world? Paul says it is a matter of renewing one's mind.

> And do not be conformed to this world, but be transformed by the renewing of your mind, that you may prove what the will of God is, that which is good and acceptable and perfect (Rom. 12:2).

We baby boomers need to have our thinking shaped by the Word of God. We specifically need to biblically renew our minds concerning our expectations. Great expectations may not indicate great faith. They may indicate great pride, great presumption, great conformity to the spirit of the world. To find out if they do, we must examine the Word of God again in three major areas: the nature of knowledge, the nature of faith, and the nature of truth.

## THE NATURE OF KNOWLEDGE

Francis Schaeffer was perhaps the first Christian writer to notice it. In his book *Escape from Reason*, published in 1968 when the first baby boomers were about to graduate from college, he noted that the so-called generation gap between parents and children was really an epistemological gap.[1] Schaeffer defined epistemology as "the theory of knowledge and the limits and validity of knowledge." To put it simply, baby boomers thought differently than their parents did. They viewed truth differently in two major areas.[2]

First, baby boomers were taught that truth is *relative*. While there was absolute truth in the hard sciences (two plus two could not equal four and five at the same time), in philosophy and religion all truth was relative. Thus, you can believe that Christ is the only way to heaven, and I can believe Muhammad is, and we both can be "right" at the same time.

Baby boomers pride themselves on being able to accept everyone's view. Please note that they champion not just everyone's right to have a view, but the rightness (validity, truth) *of* everyone's view. Your view may contradict mine, but if it's true for you, then it is "right." Truth is relative.

Mary's friend June recently joined a group that believes in the "scientific" study of Scripture. June's new approach to the Bible has caused her to reject the deity of Christ. "He is the Son of God," says June, "but Jesus is not God."

Mary believes that June's views are strange, but not incompatible with her own. "People interpret the Bible in different ways," reasons Mary. "June and I both love Jesus. That's what is important."

Second, baby boomers were taught that *experience* is the primary test of truth. If you felt good about what you believed, and it seemed to work for you, it must be true. Remember the words from Debbie Boone's song "You Light Up My Life?" "It can't be

wrong when it feels so right!" That's classic baby boom epistemology.

Mary feels the same way about June's faith. "She's happy, and
it seems to work for her," says Mary in defense.

But the Bible does not agree with the baby boom's view of truth
in either area. Biblical truth is absolute, not relative; and it, not
experience, is the primary test of truth.

There are absolute statements in the Bible. Acts 4:12 is a good
case in point. Speaking of Jesus Christ, Peter says,

> And there is salvation in no one else; for there is no other
> name under heaven that has been given among men, by
> which we must be saved (Acts 4:12).

When the apostle Peter voiced these words, he did not intend
his audience to consider them relative. He did not consider them
true for him but maybe not so for others. They were *absolutely*
true. There is salvation in no one but Jesus.

In rejecting the absolute nature of truth, baby boomers are not
only rejecting the teaching of Scripture, they are turning their
backs on traditional logic as well. Philosophers through the cen-
turies have held to the principle of contradiction as a major basis for rational thought. Simply stated, the principle says that a
statement cannot be true and false at the same time. Or, to put
it another way, if a certain thing is true, the opposite is not true.

In the area of morals the principle of contradiction would mean
that if God intended sexual relations for marriage alone, then
adultery is wrong. If telling the truth is right, then lying is wrong.
If just laws are good, then unjust laws are bad. Schaeffer says, "The
basis of classical logic is that A is A and is not non-A."[3]

In the area of theology the principle means that Jesus is either
God or He is not God. You cannot have it both ways. So either
Mary is wrong or June is.

Francis Schaeffer called this the principle of antithesis and said it is not only a necessary biblical concept but a necessary human one. It is the only way rational man can think.

> The sobering fact is that the only way one can reject thinking in terms of an antithesis and the rational is on the basis of the rational and the antithesis. When a man says that thinking in terms of an antithesis is wrong, what he is really doing is using the concept of antithesis to deny antithesis. That is the way God has made us, and there is no other way to think.[4]

But modern man, including most baby boomers, has rejected biblical and traditional rationality. The result has been intellectual and moral anarchy. No one knows any longer what is true. No one knows what is right.

Dr. Allan Bloom speaks of this anarchy in his popular book *The Closing of the American Mind*. Relativism, despite its promises to the contrary, has not opened American minds to new truths. It has only closed them to old ones. Writing of today's college student, Dr. Bloom says,

> The relativity of truth is not a theoretical insight but a moral postulate, the condition of a free society, or so they see it. They have all been equipped with this framework early on, and it is the modern replacement for the inalienable natural rights that used to be the traditional American grounds for a free society. That it is a moral issue for students is revealed by the character of their response when challenged—a combination of disbelief and indignation: "Are you an absolutist?" the only alternative they know, uttered in the same tone as "Are you a monarchist?" or "Do you really believe in witches?" This latter leads into the indignation, for

someone who believes in witches might well be a witch-hunter or a Salem judge. The danger they have been taught to fear from absolutism is not error but intolerance.[5]

Our generation's fear of intolerance is probably the reason Judge Robert Bork failed to gain Senate confirmation to the Supreme Court in the fall of 1987. The liberal left, in a well-orchestrated public relations campaign, convinced the public that Bork's absolutist view of constitutional law made him intolerant and prejudiced toward minorities. Actually, the opposite was true. Judicial activists who hold the constitution hostage to the changing values of society are the ones responsible for the kind of intolerance that has sacrificed the lives of millions of unborn babies on the altar of their mothers' freedom of choice. Dr. Bloom continues,

> Relativism is necessary to openness; and this is the virtue, the only virtue, which all primary education for more than fifty years has dedicated itself to inculcating. Openness—and the relativism that makes it the only plausible stance in the face of various claims to truth and various ways of life and kinds of human beings—is the great insight of our times. The true believer is the real danger. The study of history and of culture teaches that all the world was mad in the past; men always thought they were right, and that led to wars, persecutions, slavery, xenophobia, racism, and chauvinism. The point is not to correct the mistakes and really be right; rather it is not to think you are right at all.[6]

And too many Christian baby boomers have bought the concept. Most have not bought the relativism that affects values and cheapens human life, but they have bought a relativism that affects theology and weakens biblical faith. Christian leaders have taught that when the Bible says God's wisdom is foolishness to man, it means that God's wisdom is nonrational. With God, A can equal non-A. The Bible can be self-contradictory and still be true. God's truth is relative.

But God does not violate His own laws of reality, including the principle of contradiction. Man thinks as he does because God thinks as He does. We are made in His image. He is not self-contradictory. He is consistent with His own nature. The Scripture says of Him, "There is no variation or shifting shadow" (James 1:17) and "God is not a man, that He should lie" (Num. 23:19).

The major problem posed by Christian baby boomers who reject rational thought has come in the area of hermeneutics. Hermeneutics is the discipline of interpreting Scripture. We must interpret Scripture rationally. With the help of the Holy Spirit we use normal laws of grammar, knowledge of culture and history, and basic laws of logic to interpret the Scripture as the writers meant for us to do.

Is June's "scientific" method of interpreting Scripture really rational? Does it give the meaning intended by the original writers? Or is it simply a smokescreen for those who would bend sound doctrine to their own desires? (See 2 Timothy 4:3.)

You see, the Bible teaches that we all have a right to interpret Scripture for ourselves (1 John 2:27). It does not teach that all our interpretations are right. It is possible to adulterate the Word of God (2 Cor. 4:2). Some distort Scriptures to their own destruction (2 Pet. 3:16). No Scripture is "a matter of one's own interpretation" (2 Pet. 1:20).

Yet baby boomers often develop unbiblical expectations because they wrongly interpret verses of Scripture. Sometimes the false expectations come in major doctrinal areas, as with June's view of the deity of Christ. But more often they come in more minor, yet still important, areas such as God's leading in our own daily lives.

Ed has been diagnosed with terminal lung cancer. In his Bible reading his eyes fall on Deuteronomy 7:15: "The LORD will remove from you all sickness." He takes this as assurance of his imminent healing.

Carol is involved in a custody hearing for her child. Thumbing through the Bible on the day of the trial she reads Deuteronomy 28:7: "The LORD will cause your enemies who rise up against you to be defeated before you." She believes God gave her this verse to assure her of victory in the courtroom.

Ted is in line for a promotion at work. During the week a position becomes available, he reads Deuteronomy 28:13 in his quiet time. "The LORD shall make you the head and not the tail, and you only shall be above." He believes this is God's promise of his impending promotion.

It is true that God does give us verses to help in daily living. The Scripture is profitable. God does not, however, violate His own rules of logic to do so. If your expectation does not fit the normal meaning of the verse, you have no reason to believe it has been given to you by God.

And in context all the promises just mentioned are directed to the Jewish people as they enter the land of Canaan under Joshua. They are not directly applicable to the church. They are not specific promises to you and me. God may grant us healing, vindication, or promotion, but on the basis of these verses, we have no right to expect Him *always* to do so. Faith comes by hearing, and hearing by the Word of Christ, properly interpreted.

Similarly, biblical writers promoted the Scripture, not experience, as the *primary* test of truth. Galatians 1:8-9 is a good example.

> But even though we, or an angel from heaven, should preach to you a gospel contrary to that which we have preached to you, let him be accursed.
>
> As we have said before, so I say again now, if any man is preaching to you a gospel contrary to that which you received, let him be accursed.

The place of experience as a primary test of truth in these verses is conspicuous by its absence. Paul does not say to give other gospels a chance to see how they work. He does not ask us to pray about them and then see if we "feel" they are true.

Most major cults in our day rely heavily on experience as the test of truth. They point to the large numbers of people who are joining their movement. They highlight the positive affects their teaching has on society. They describe their "burning in the bosom" that convinced them of the truth of their faith.

Yet Paul would have none of that. The gospel is not negotiable, and the primary test is Scripture itself. If it is a different gospel than the one Scripture proclaims, then it is not *the* gospel, and the one peddling it is a heretic. Paul's own experience confirmed his beliefs about God and Christ, true, but the final criterion for truth was not experience but God's Word.

Experience is, after all, a pretty shaky test of truth, especially in the short run. Do you remember Jesus' parable of the sower? In Jesus' story a farmer inadvertently scatters some seed on rocky places and it "immediately sprang up." Now, a novice farmer might have thought rocks were the answer to the need for increased productivity. After all, the results were there for all to see. No other ground produced such quick growth.

Yet seasoned farmers would know better. They know that plants will sprout quickly in rocky soil because they do not first grow down and develop a good root system. They would know that the results would be short-lived. "But when the sun had risen they were scorched; and because they had no root, they withered away" (Matt. 13:6).

Baby boomers need to learn the lesson of this parable. Too often we have let superficial experience shape our theology. We need to let our sound theology interpret our experience, not vice versa. Only then can we tell the difference between fruit that will fade and fruit that will last.

You see, baby boom believers have been victimized by false

religious teachers who raised their expectations to false heights by false epistemology.

If truth is relative and experience is the primary test, I can go on TV and tell you God met with me out on a remote hilltop and gave me the keys to financial success. Then if I'm driving a Jaguar and living in a half-million-dollar home—and for good measure I throw in a few out-of-context Scripture verses—who are you to argue?

The Book of Acts says the believers at Berea were more noble-minded "for they received the word with great eagerness, examining the Scriptures daily, to see whether these things were so" (Acts 17:11). Baby boom believers would do well to become like the Bereans. We need a biblical epistemology. The Bible itself must become our supreme test of truth.

By the way, the Berean test was one of expectations. They expected the Christ to come. Paul said that He had come. The text says he

> reasoned with them from the Scriptures, explaining and giving evidence that the Christ had to suffer and rise again from the dead, and saying, "This Jesus whom I am proclaiming to you is the Christ" (Acts 17:23).

And the Bereans searched the Scriptures to see if Paul's words should alter their own expectations. Some of them "were persuaded" that they should. Baby boomers need to do the same with contemporary religious teachers. Are their expectations biblical? If so, we follow them. If not, even though they claim God has spoken to them, their teaching must be rejected. Like Paul, those of us who proclaim the Word of God today must prove our teaching is in harmony with that Word.

And what is true for teachers is also true for individuals. Anne believes God has given her psychic abilities. She believes she can sometimes read minds and predict future events. She also is convinced she has seen and communicated with departed spirits. Some of Anne's predictions have come true. Many have not. Most are too general to really determine their accuracy.

Anne says she is a Christian. What about her claims? Are they valid expectations? What basis does she have for saying she communicates with the dead? Who decides? What does Scripture say? The last question must be answered.

## THE NATURE OF FAITH

*Faith* is, in the Bible, a loaded word. It is rich in meaning. It is one of the greatest words in the Christian vocabulary. But *faith* is not so meaningful in the secular world. It is vague, shallow. To secular baby boomers, faith is simply a positive mental attitude. The power of faith is the power of positive thinking. The mind is a powerful tool able to work the miraculous in our lives. "Whatever you can conceive, you can achieve." Like the Little Engine That Could, we can achieve by saying, "I think I can; I think I can," and, for many people, that is faith.

Religious teachers of our era have simply brought this teaching over to Christianity, baptizing it with some verses from the Bible. Faith is what the Bible means, we are told, when it says, "As a man thinks in his heart, so is he." (Actually, that verse — Proverbs 22:6 — has more to say about the deceitfulness of outward appearances than it does about positive thinking.)

While there is some truth to positive thinking — how we think *does* have a great effect on how we act — it is not equivalent to biblical faith. Positive thinking falls short in two major areas. One, it does not differentiate between faith and presumption. And two, it emphasizes the quantity rather than the quality of faith.

The Bible distinguishes between true faith and presumption. In Numbers 14 the children of Israel rebel against God at a place called Kadesh-Barnea. Instead of following Moses into the

Promised Land, they balk at the prospects of facing the "giants in the land." Cloaking their own cowardice with words of concern for their children ("the land will devour them"), they decide to return to Egypt.

Then God appears to them and threatens total destruction. Moses intercedes, and God pardons their sin. He will not destroy them immediately, but all the fighting men aged twenty and older will not be allowed to enter the land of Canaan. Instead, they will wander in the wilderness for almost forty years until their unbelieving generation has all died.

There were only two exceptions to God's judgment—Joshua and Caleb, the only two warriors who had argued along with Moses for invading the land and conquering the giants. They would be spared and would one day possess the land.

When Moses spoke these words to the people, they "mourned greatly." They did not, however, repent.

> In the morning, however, they rose up early and went up to the ridge of the hill country, saying, "Here we are; we have indeed sinned, but we will go up to the place which the LORD has promised."
>
> But Moses said, "Why then are you transgressing the commandment of the LORD, when it will not succeed? Do not go up, lest you be struck down before your enemies, for the LORD is not among you. For the Amalekites and the Canaanites will be there in front of you, and you will fall by the sword, inasmuch as you have turned back from following the LORD. And the LORD will not be with you."
>
> But they went up heedlessly to the ridge of the hill country; neither the ark of the covenant of the LORD nor Moses left the camp.
>
> Then the Amalekites and the Canaanites who lived in that hill country came down, and struck them and beat them down as far as Hormah (Num. 14:40-45).

The rebellious Hebrews did not lack for PMA (positive mental attitude). They believed they could be successful even without Moses. Perhaps they believed he had misinterpreted God's word. Didn't they have a right to their own interpretation? Or maybe they thought God would change His mind in view of their new "courage."

But God did not change His mind, and they received their own expectation bust. Remember Jesus' words, "He who exalts himself will be humbled." Who says you can't have it all? The God of reality, that's who.

The Bible says they acted heedlessly or presumptuously. Their PMA was a presumptuous mental attitude. But true faith is acting on what God has promised. If they had invaded the land a day earlier, they would have been successful. Presumption, then, is acting on what God has *not* promised. And no amount of positive mental attitude can circumvent the negative results. You cannot achieve everything you can conceive—not if what you conceive is outside of the moral will of God!

Baby boom believers have often exercised presumption rather than faith. We have entertained great expectations of financial independence, of comfortable and painless living, of quick and easy spiritual victories, and of a Christian entitlement to enjoy the visible trappings of success in the world.

We have intensely held these expectations, believing that merely holding to them fervently (our PMA) would help bring them about. Yet for most of us such has not been the case. Like the Hebrews at Kadesh-Barnea, we have been humbled. Such will normally be the experience of an overexpecter. Whether we presumptuously seek the seats of honor at a banquet table or in life, those who exalt themselves will be humbled.

One night Rick heard the "voice of God." He had just gone to bed after staying up late to watch a real estate seminar on cable TV. The program was entitled "How to Make Millions in Real Estate Using Other People's Money."

Rick sensed an inner voice telling him to quit his job at the post office and become an investor in real estate. The next day he did, and soon he and many of his friends had invested heavily, often with borrowed money, in a booming real estate market.

Six months later Rick and his friends were broke. The market had collapsed. Rick would have done much better to have listened to the written Word of God rather than an inner voice he thought was the spoken word of God. Scripture could have helped him avoid an unwise decision.

> He who tills his land will
>     have plenty of food,
> But he who follows empty
>     *pursuits* will
>     have poverty in plenty.
>
> A faithful man will
>     abound with blessings,
> But he who makes haste to be
>     rich will not go unpunished.
> (Prov. 28:19-20)

Second, viewing faith as merely a positive mental attitude wrongly emphasizes the quantity of faith rather than its quality. It's the intensity of faith that is stressed. How hard do you believe something? How sincere are you?

But Jesus taught that great faith is qualitative not quantitative. It was not how much faith you had, but in whom.

> If you have faith as a mustard seed, you shall say to this mountain, "Move from here to there," and it shall move; and nothing shall be impossible to you (Matt. 17:20).

The disciples wanted Jesus to increase their faith. Perhaps they thought of faith quantitatively and thus they wanted more of it, more PMA. But according to Jesus, you don't need mountains of faith; the mustard seed variety (very small) will do just fine. What you need to do is place that *mustard seed* faith in a *mountain-moving* God! That's the key to great faith.

Emphasizing faith's intensity in our day has glorified man, not God. When you see me pull up in my old run-down car and comment on my great faith in that car, you may have paid me a compliment. But what have you said about my car, the object of my faith?

Similarly, when you see some religious celebrity complimented on a TV talk show for his or her great faith which has inspired all of us, it is usually not God who is being complimented.

If you want to compliment someone on his great faith (thinking quantitatively), don't compliment the Christian. Instead, compliment the naturalistic microevolutionist. To believe that life came from non-life, that person came from non-person, that the specialness and orderliness of our universe just happened over billions of years by coincidence—that takes great faith.

Or compliment the secular humanist. To believe man is basically good and getting better by his own efforts, in the face of all the evidence to the contrary—that takes great faith.

But should we compliment the believer in God? Does it take great faith to believe in a God who has never failed, not once, who has never broken a promise? On the contrary, given the right data, it takes great stupidity and rebelliousness not to believe in such a God!

Baby boomers need to stop working so hard on the intensity of faith (quantity) and instead start working on its content (quality). It wasn't their strong feelings of belief that made great the faith of our fathers. They didn't have great PMA.

In fact, sometimes their feelings were quite negative—"I was with you in weakness and in fear and in much trembling" (1 Cor. 2:3). Yet they believed in a God who could use even weak men to accomplish His purposes. And, as a result, their faith did "not rest on the wisdom of men, but on the power of God" (1 Cor. 2:5). Their secret was not mountains of faith, but a mountain-moving God.

## THE NATURE OF BIBLICAL TRUTH

We baby boomers have fallen victim to the proponents of religious success gospels, and thus have had our expectations raised too high, because we have failed to understand the nature of biblical truth. Specifically, we have not distinguished between what is significant and what is exhaustive.

The apostle Paul says, "All Scripture is inspired by God and profitable for teaching, for reproof, for correction, for training in righteousness" (2 Tim. 3:16).

All biblical truth is significant. It is all profitable. Even the genealogies, Old Testament laws, and historical passages have practical value. They were recorded to reprove, correct, and instruct us.

Yet all biblical passages are not exhaustive. That is, few, if any, say *all* the Bible has to say on a given subject. Thus they are part of the truth, but not all of the truth. And many, if taken by themselves and used to advance a false teaching, can be misleading. Perhaps this is part of what Paul meant when he referred to those who walk in craftiness and adulterate the Word of God.

A sample verse will help to illustrate the point.

When a man's ways are pleasing to the LORD,
He makes even his enemies to be at peace with him (Prov. 16:7).

This is significant biblical truth. It is "profitable for training in righteousness." Our relationship with God has a profound effect on our relationships with men. Peace with God will often bring peace with men.

However, the truth is not exhaustive. The verse does not say his enemies will *always* be at peace with him. A good relationship with God does not *guarantee* a good relationship with men.

To prove the point one need only remember Jesus Christ. His ways always pleased the Father; therefore, many former enemies did seek peace with Him. Yet some remained enemies. Some even crucified Him.

Here's another example: "And all things you ask in prayer, believing, you shall receive" (Matt. 21:22).

This is significant biblical truth. It follows, incidentally, the verse on "mustard seed" faith. If you believe in the God who can move mountains, it will transform your prayer life. There will not be any circumstance considered too hard for God. You will dare to ask the naturally impossible.

But does the verse mean I can ask for *anything* and receive it just as long as I believe? What if I ask for a new BMW so I can keep up my yuppie image and feel good about myself?

The apostle James might have a word to say to me if I did. "You ask and do not receive, because you ask with wrong motives, so that you may spend it on your pleasures" (James 4:3).

And James is not the only biblical writer to set down other criteria for effective prayer. To get the whole truth on the subject we must listen to all of them.

By making significant truth exhaustive, baby boom believers have come up with all kinds of unrealistic and *unbiblical* expectations. For instance some have taught that God always wants you prosperous and popular.

Others teach that Jesus always wants you well. With enough faith, they say, healing will always follow.

Some say wayward children or spouses always result from bad parents or mates.

And some say you can bring about anyone's salvation if only you pray and believe hard enough—a feat, incidentally, that God does not even claim for Himself (see Matt. 23:37.)

Perhaps the greatest tragedy of these unbiblical expectations is their effect on the ones holding them. A man who is already suffering intensely with a terminal illness does not need the added burden of guilt because he does not have "the faith" to be cured. A hurting divorcee who sincerely tried to make her marriage work does not need to be told that it would have if only she had submitted more to her abusive and unfaithful husband.

God is our Father, and He is perfect. Yet, as His children, we sometimes rebel. Does our rebellion mean He is not a good parent? No, and neither does the rebellion of natural children necessarily reflect bad parenting. God has given both them and us a free will. We can expect that good parenting will normally lead to maturing children. We cannot expect it to always do so.

Sam is one of about 80 percent of all American pastors who serve a congregation of a hundred people or less. He is also a baby boomer in his mid-thirties. His expectations for successful ministry were formed from watching Billy Graham crusades on TV.

Last year Sam attended Brother Jake Edward's highly touted seminar on church growth and expansion. Brother Jake's enthusiasm at the meetings was contagious, and Sam returned to his rural pastorate with the goal of seeing his own flock increase tenfold (from sixty to six hundred) in just ten years.

Sam met with early success as his board of deacons decided to join him in "a renewed assault on the demons of unbelief and apathy." They named their objective (ten new families per month) and claimed their victory.

As an "act of faith" they even released the six thousand dollars in the building fund, money given for capital improvements two years ago when dear old Mrs. Morrison went to be with the Lord. "She would want it this way," they reasoned. "We will use the money for Brother Jake's famous media-blitz evangelism," said Sam. "With all the new people joining us, it will be no time at all before we replenish the building fund."

Six months and six thousand dollars later the church is still hovering at around sixty people. The media blitz did bring some new people, but most of them left. Along with them went several of the regulars who didn't like Sam's "new direction for the church."

Even the deacons are no longer supportive. As one of them sarcastically remarked, "Sam brought home Brother Jake's methods but not his faith." Sam is disillusioned and ready to quit. He has a job interview this week with an insurance agency. "At least there people will appreciate my extra effort," explains Sam.

## THE DEMAND FOR CERTAINTY

Perhaps one reason sincere Christians have tried to make significant truth exhaustive is because of their belief that faith is positive thinking. Christian positive thinkers like to have verses that say all there is to say on a particular topic. If they don't, they lose the attitude of certainty which they see as necessary to real faith.

For instance, Matthew 21:22 must be taken to mean that the *only* requirement for answered prayer is belief. But if you add to this verse the passages that suggest the need for praying according to God's will, or with proper motives, you inject a feeling of uncertainty into your prayer. (Am I sure this is God's will? Am I sure my motives are pure?) Such uncertainty is unacceptable to positive thinkers. To them, an attitude of uncertainty is an attitude of unbelief. To pray with faith, they must be able to pray with complete certainty, and to pray with certainty, they must know for sure what the specific will of God is in the matter.

They must believe for sure that God is going to heal their disease, or that God is going to bring back their mate, or that God is going to prosper them financially. Please note, it is important for them to know not just that God *can* do these things, or that He *desires* to do these things. They must also know that He *does* do these things, always, under all circumstances, if only they believe. In other words, the prayers of these people presuppose that God acts in a mechanical fashion. One plus one equals two. My real faith plus God's reliability equals the results I want.

How different these prayers are from the one our Lord spoke in the garden of Gethsemane. We are told He fell on His face before the Father and prayed: "My Father, if it is possible, let this cup pass from Me; yet not as I will, but as Thou wilt" (Matt. 26:39).

Jesus was definitely not a positive thinker in the modern mold. If He had been, He would probably have rephrased the petition to exclude His uncertainty: "Father, I know it is possible for this cup to pass. I am believing it to be so. I right now claim my deliverance. Thank you, Father, for the victory!"

But Jesus prayed no such prayer. He could not do so with certainty. And often in our own experiences, neither can you and I. We may know that God *can* answer our prayer. We may also know that such a request is consistent with His character. It is something that under normal circumstances He would *desire* to do for us.

But we do not know that He *will* do it. For reasons known only to Him, it may not be within His sovereign will. Sometimes like our Savior we can pray only: "Father, if it is possible . . . yet not as I will, but as Thou wilt."

By the way, uncertain prayers are not necessarily unproductive prayers. Acts 12 illustrates the concept. Herod Agrippa had just executed James, the brother of John, and he intended to do the same with the apostle Peter. But while Peter awaited execution in his prison cell, "prayer for him was being made fervently by the church to God" (Acts 12:5).

Question: How certain were these fervent and productive prayers? How certain was the church that God would, in fact, deliver Peter?

The answer is that they were not very certain at all. In fact, when

God sent an angel to deliver him, Peter himself "did not know that what was being done by the angel was real, but thought he was seeing a vision" (Acts 12:9). Peter obviously did not expect to be set free. He thought he was dreaming.

And those who were praying for him were even less sure of the outcome. When Peter showed up at the site of their prayer meeting, and when a servant girl named Rhoda announced Peter's arrival, the words of these early believers showed anything but certainty.

> And they said to her, "You are out of your mind!" But she kept insisting that it was so. And they kept saying, "It is his angel" (Acts 12:15).

"Either you are insane or you've seen a ghost," they told Rhoda. By the way, Rhoda was the only certain person at that prayer meeting. And she was certain not because she had faith but because she had eyes. She had seen Peter at the door. Soon they all shared her visual certainty. The text says, "They saw him and were amazed."

That's the way prayer is. You don't have to expect a miracle to get one—not when you serve a God "who is able to do exceeding abundantly beyond all that we ask or think" (Eph. 3:20).

So don't give up on prayer because you lack certainty. After all, your faith is not in your positive mental attitude but in the God who can move mountains. With Him mustard seed faith is all you need.

So by demanding certainty in our prayers we may not have encouraged faith at all. Rather we may have encouraged dishonesty or presumption. We may have encouraged believers to lie to God or to try to bully Him into doing what they wish. Both are wrong and dangerous actions. And they, rather than an attitude of uncertainty, are unproductive.

Thus understanding the nature of knowledge, the nature of faith, and the nature of truth is the foundation for biblical expectations. It will help us discard the worldly expectations of our era. Now we are ready to replace them with what the Bible really teaches.

# 5

*Real People:
Facing the Reality
of the Struggle*

Biblical heroes were real people with real struggles. The great men and women of God were not unaffected by such things as fear, anger, lust, depression and prejudice. In fact, the Bible's candor regarding its heroes is one of its most convincing proofs of divine inspiration. Had not God Himself superintended its human writers, surely the Bible would not record so vividly the real failures of its famous personalities.

For instance, we would read of Abraham leaving all security to follow God into a strange land, but we would never know of the fear which made him offer to sacrifice his wife's sexual purity—not once but twice—to save his own neck.

We would know that Moses was mighty in words and deeds, but not that his bad temper once resulted in murder and ultimately kept him from entering the Promised Land.

David would still be known as the man after God's own heart. Left unwritten would be the story of his losing battle with lust.

Elijah would still be remembered for his great victory over the prophets of Baal. However, we would never know of the depths of his mental depression only hours later.

Peter would be remembered as the first Jewish leader to enthusiastically welcome Gentiles into the church at Caesarea. Left unwritten would be the resurgence of his prejudice some years later at Antioch.

And the list could go on and on. If mere men had written the Bible apart from divine inspiration, surely we would not hear them admit to the saints' moral inconsistencies and intense struggles.

So why did God choose to record the lives of His most famous servants realistically, warts and all? Perhaps He wants us to form realistic expectations of the Christian life.

He wants us to know that changes do come in our lives. (After all, He is molding us into the image of Christ.) These changes do not, however, come instantly or easily. Nor are they always permanent. There is, even for the most mature believer, a real struggle in the Christian life.

Herein lies the problem with the Cinderella-type testimony of some of today's Christian authors. They would have us believe that victory in the Christian life comes easily, instantly, and permanently. The problem is that while their words may be inspiring, they are not inspired—not in the same way the Bible is. Their words are not reliable in the same sense that Scripture is reliable. They are missing the Holy Spirit's guarantee of their accuracy. He has not laid bare their failures for all to see. Biblical writers had no such luxury.

Romans 7 is a case in point. Sandwiched between Paul's words on the high standing of the believer in Romans 6 and his description of our victorious walk in the Spirit in Romans 8 is this passage which gives the human context for the victory God gives us. Romans 7 makes it painfully clear that believers—even the great ones like Paul—continue to struggle with sin. Frankly, this passage would be best omitted by the overexpecter. It just doesn't fit the neatly wrapped package of the Cinderella-type testimony.

In fact, some have tried to do just that—omit the chapter altogether. They do so not by denying its textual integrity, but by relegating it to a past experience in the life of Paul. "Either these verses describe Paul as an unbeliever," we are told, "or they show him before he learned the victory of chapter 8."

But honest exegesis will simply not allow the omission. The verbs describing his struggle include not only past but present tenses. And in his concluding statement in verse 25, he both affirms the victory in the first part of the verse, and reaffirms the present-tense struggle in the last part.

No, Paul was describing his present situation, not his condition in years past. Chapter 7 speaks of the struggle he faced trying to combine the theory of chapter 6 with the practice of chapter 8.

Here, in a brief and frank autobiographical sketch, Paul tells us why he struggled. But it is not just his story. It is ours. Here is the reality of your struggle and mine.

Two things, says Paul, contribute to our struggle.

> For while we were in the flesh, the sinful passions, which were aroused by the Law, were at work in the members of our body to bear fruit for death (Rom. 7:5).

Did you spot the two essential ingredients in our struggle? We struggle in the Christian life because of the sinful passions and because of the Law.

The Law, says Paul, defines sin.

> What shall we say then? Is the Law sin? May it never be! On the contrary, I would not have come to know sin except through the Law; for I would not have known about coveting if the Law had not said, "You shall not covet" (Rom. 7:7).

This is not classic baby boom epistemology. Sin, in the biblical view, is not relative. It does not depend on how we feel about it or whether it *feels* bad for us. The Law of God tells us what sin is. Coveting—wanting that which belongs to another—is sin.

But the Law does not only define sin, it provokes sin. Paul would not have known coveting if the Law had not helped him, but the struggle did not end there.

> But sin, taking opportunity through the commandment, produced in me coveting of every kind; for apart from the Law sin is dead (Rom. 7:8).

Apart from the Law's influence, sin is dead or dormant. Remember the essential elements of our struggle in verse five? The sinful passions, are *aroused* by the Law.

How does the phenomenon work? Perhaps a modern-day illustration will help. The baby boom's entrance into adulthood not only greatly increased our nation's suicide rate, it brought an unprecedented boom in the crime rate. In the decade from 1960 to 1970, the number of violent crimes jumped by 10 percent a year. At the same time robberies were growing by 18 percent a year. Chances are now almost one in two that you will be robbed sometime in your lifetime. This wasn't true for your parents or grandparents.

Suppose you decide to prevent such an occurrence. However, instead of buying a good alarm system or a Doberman, you spend your money on signs. You erect a large billboard in your front yard that reads "Do Not Take Valuables from This Property." Maybe you even get specific: "Do Not Take My VCR, Mink Coat, or Diamond Ring."

How effective do you think your sign would be in preventing crime? Would it make you less likely to be robbed? What would potential thieves think as they drove by your house?

They would probably think the same as did the apostle Paul after reading the law about coveting and then passing by his neighbor's place.

"I wonder what my neighbor has that I might want. Oh, I see. Yes, I might want that ox. Sure looks like a nice animal. Would look good hitched to my new wagon. Why can't I have it? After all, my neighbor has another, and I deserve it more than he does. Who is he to tell me I can't have it anyway? I can do darn well what I please!"

Yes, the Law, good and fair though it is, is like that. It arouses sinful passions. It provokes us to rebel. It brings sin to life.

Next, Paul says, the Law condemns and brings death.

> And I was once alive apart from the Law; but when the commandment came, sin became alive, and I died; and this commandment, which was to result in life, proved to result in death for me; for sin, taking opportunity through the commandment, deceived me, and through it killed me (Rom. 7:9-11).

Paul does not speak here of mere physical death. Death and life in the Bible are qualitative terms. Eternal life is not just more existence. It is a kind of life, a quality of life filled with things like joy, peace, and love. And it will last forever in heaven. Death, on the other hand, is the opposite, an existence filled with things like envy, resentment, and despair. Hell will be like that.

Paul had looked to the Old Testament Law to give him life. He wanted to please God, to learn what sin was so he could avoid it. But the Law not only defines sin, it arouses it, and Paul suffered an expectation bust. He ended up sinning more than in the first place. He experienced the deathlike qualities of overwhelming guilt and despair.

Do you sense the disillusionment in his words? Have you ever tried something which promised to help you, maybe at great personal expense and sacrifice, and then had the product fail to produce the desired results?

Joy felt this disillusionment a few weeks after attending a

seminar sponsored by her church. The seminar was entitled "How to Win over Worry—Eight Easy Steps to Emotional Freedom." Joy read the brochures announcing the series with great anticipation. Worry was her Achilles' heel, her most besetting sin. If only she could gain victory over it, then she could get on with life.

But to say the seminar failed to live up to its billing and Joy's expectations is an understatement. The speaker's mixture of pop psychology, mind control, and relaxation techniques did little to solve her problem with worry. Even the Scripture verses scattered somewhat infrequently through the talks didn't help. The steps the speaker described all seemed to depend on her own mental capabilities to stop worrying, abilities which the speaker said were unlimited but which Joy knew were exhausted.

Why did the seminar not work for Joy? More important, why did the Law not work for Paul? After all, Paul affirms in verse 12 that God's Law is holy, righteous, and good. The problem, Paul concludes in verse 11, is sin, not the Law.

> For we know that the Law is spiritual; but I am of flesh, sold into bondage to sin (Rom. 7:14).

Can you identify with Paul? He wants to keep the Law, to do what is right, but he feels enslaved to sin.

> For that which I am doing, I do not understand; for I am not practicing what I would like to do, but I am doing the very thing I hate. For the good that I wish, I do not do; but I practice the very evil I do not wish (Rom. 7:15, 19).

Sound like the words of anyone you know? Do you ever fail to understand your own actions? Do you ever hurt those you love most? Do you do something that hurts yourself, promise yourself you'll never do it again, and then do it again and again? Do you ever plan one type of behavior and end up doing another?

Renee is probably nodding with understanding if she is read-ing these words. She knows all too well what it feels like to do the thing one hates. Renee is suffering from bulimia, a malady which has been epidemic among young baby boom women. She has become enslaved to a food disorder in which one first binges (greatly overeats), then purges (gets rid of the food through in-ducing vomiting or taking laxatives).

Widespread in today's society, bulimia is largely the result of our generation's obsession with thinness. The bulimic, almost always an overexpecting female, tries to control at least this one area of life through a method that has proven effective. The prob-lem is that the new master, bulimia, is worse than the old mas-ter, perceived obesity; and the controller becomes the controlled. Renee can identify with Paul. She is no longer a master, but a slave.

Wouldn't it be nice if good could be accomplished just by wish-ing? Don't we wish hard for changes in our lives? But mere wishes didn't work for Paul, and they don't often work for us either. It almost seems as though we have some kind of wish-blockers hid-ing out in our bodies. Maybe we do.

> So now, no longer am I the one doing it, but sin which in-dwells me.
>
> For I know that nothing good dwells in me, that is, in my flesh; for the wishing is present in me but the doing of the good is not.
>
> For the good that I wish, I do not do; but I practice the very evil that I do not wish. But if I am doing the very thing I do not wish, I am no longer the one doing it, but sin which dwells in me (Rom. 7:17-20).

There was a wish-blocker in Paul's life. He calls it sin and says it dwells in him. The Greek word translated "dwell" means "to be at home in." This wish-blocker, sin, is at home in Paul's body.

Do you know what I think of when I read Paul's words? I think of the dandelions in my yard, those pretty yellow wildflowers that, despite repeated sprayings and diggings, continue to show up in my Bermuda grass year after year after year.

They are "at home" in my yard. They were here before me, and I'm sure they will be around long after I leave. Sin is like that in our human bodies. We have in us a wish-blocker which rebels against the Law of God. It can be exposed, explained, and condemned, even temporarily controlled. But until God one day gives us new bodies, it will never be eradicated.

Thus Paul has a civil war going on in his own body.

> I find then the principle that evil is present in me, the one who wishes to do good.
>
> For I joyfully concur with the Law of God in the inner man, but I see a different law in the members of my body, waging war against the Law of my mind, and making me a prisoner of the Law of sin which is in my members (Rom. 7:21-23).

Do you sometimes feel pulled in different directions? Does part of you want to do good, to keep on the diet, to be kind and respectful to your unkind boss, to refuse sexual temptation? But another side of you, a part of you that you hope no one else knows about, refuses to easily submit to your good intentions. In fact, it often wins the struggle. Paul is right. It is a war. Isn't it?

No wonder Paul exclaims in verse 24: "Wretched man that I am! Who will set me free from the body of this death?"

The Greek word translated "wretched" means "to bear a callous." It seems to Paul that sin has heaped ugly scar tissue on his soul. He is filled with self-hatred. Who will deliver him?

It is a perceptive question. He does not ask *what* will deliver, but *Who?* Paul has tried the "whats" in life. He even tried the Law of God, but as 1 Timothy 1:8 and Romans 7 show, there are certain things the Law cannot do. (See accompanying chart.)

The righteous Law cannot depose sin. It cannot make sin decrease. It cannot save us or impart life to us. It cannot justify or sanctify, and it cannot give spiritual freedom. Why can it not do these things? Paul says in Romans 8:3 that the Law is "weak through the flesh." The Law depends on us; and we, like Paul, know how wretched we are.

But the Law can do some things. It can define sin. It can condemn to punishment and lead to death. So why did God give the Law? Why did He lay down rules against which He knew we would rebel, and before which sensitive people would feel wretched?

> Therefore the Law has become our tutor to lead us to Christ, that we may be justified by faith (Gal. 3:24).

God gave the Law to bring Paul and you and me to the very point of desperation Paul shows in Romans 7. The Law shows us the need for a Savior. And it shows the necessity of receiving Him by faith. Wretched men can't save or sanctify themselves. They cannot approach God by works.

This is another of the problems with viewing faith as mere positive thinking. Paul could not get his act together by just thinking more positively. The problem was not simply that he *thought* himself too wretched. His problem and ours is that we *are* too wretched.

At this point in Romans 7 most commentators will proceed to explain the life of faith, how to walk in the Spirit a la Romans 8. The assumption seems to be that if you do that, the struggle of Romans 7 is over. You've discovered the Christian's "secret of a happy life." "Welcome to the palace, Cinderella!"

But Romans 7 is the prelude for the victory of Romans 8. Paul obviously knew the principles of Romans 8 when he described his struggle in Romans 7. Yes, "the Spirit of life in Christ Jesus does set us free from the Law of sin and death," but, realistically, this victory does not come in a struggle-free vacuum. It is neither easy, instant, nor permanent—not in this life, anyway.

Before hurrying to the truths of Romans 8, and they are wonderfully liberating truths, we need to learn the lessons of Romans 7. There are at least three major ones.

First, we cannot gain standing with God nor can we grow significantly in the Christian life by the Law system. The Law is good, but it depends too much on the flesh which is often wretched. This is the weakness of self-help programs. They are only as good as we make them, and too often that's not good enough.

This does not mean we live lawlessly under grace. God's righteousness expressed in the Law is still our goal. It does mean that we cannot depend on ourselves alone to pull it off. God must work in us "both to will and to work for His good pleasure" (Phil. 2:13).

The Law can only be liberating (see James 1:25) when it is written not merely with ink "but with the Spirit of the living God, not on tablets of stone, but on tablets of human hearts" (2 Cor. 3:3).

Second, we do not struggle alone. Life is often hard, brutal, and tragic. Christian victory does not come easily. Our struggle is often intense. But we are not alone. Paul wrestled with the same internal battles we face. Ditto for the other heroes of the faith. We dare not give up simply because righteousness does not come easily.

Third, we do not struggle without hope. We are not only wretched people in a sinful world. We are, more importantly, new creatures in Christ. Romans 7 is a prelude to Romans 8, and "if God is for us who can be against us." The Holy Spirit "helps our infirmities." Paul struggled greatly. He also was greatly used of God. His struggles did not disqualify him for effective service.

That's why Paul, in spite of his understanding of human wretchedness, expressed great confidence in the future growth and maturity of his disciples.

For I am confident of this very thing, that He who began a good work in you will perfect it until the day of Christ Jesus (Phil. 1:6).

Paul knew that those whom God foreknew (all believers) He also "predestined to be conformed to the image of His Son" (Rom. 8:29). And "faithful is He who calls you, and He also will bring it to pass" (1 Thess. 5:24).

God fights for us in the Christian walk. He is committed to our ultimate Christ-likeness. In fact, sometimes He fights for us by fighting against us. When we consistently disobey, He disciplines us so "that we may not be condemned along with the world" (1 Cor. 11:32). Even discipline is for our good. What a comforting thought for those of us who struggle!

It is expecting too little not to expect changes in your behavior as you grow in Christ. God is committed to your sanctification. The Holy Spirit will fulfill "the requirement of the Law" in us (Rom. 8:4). On the other hand, it is expecting too much to think that change will come without a struggle. There is no quick and easy victory.

What will happen if we expect too much here? Practically speaking, is it all that damaging to deny the reality of our continuing struggle as believers?

Yes, it is damaging. Our overexpectations will always be self-defeating. One who expects not to struggle in the Christian walk has only two choices. One, he can become a hypocrite, or two, he may drop out of the race altogether.

The Pharisees were prime examples of religious people who denied their struggle. Jesus used them as examples to teach His disciples the necessity of admitting their own sinfulness.

Two men went up into the temple to pray, one a Pharisee, and the other a tax-gatherer.

The Pharisee stood and was praying thus to himself, "God, I thank Thee that I am not like other people: swindlers, unjust, adulterers, or even like this tax-gatherer. I fast twice a week; I pay tithes of all that I get."

But the tax-gatherer, standing some distance away, was even unwilling to lift up his eyes to heaven, but was beating his breast, saying, "God, be merciful to me, the sinner!"

I tell you, this man went down to his house justified rather than the other; for everyone who exalts himself shall be humbled, but he who humbles himself shall be exalted (Luke 18:10-14).

The Greek word translated "hypocrite" in our English Bible means "to be an actor on a stage, to play a part." Those who deny their ongoing struggles in the Christian life do so at the expense of their own integrity. They must fake it. They are hypocrites.

On the other hand, having a biblical and realistic view of your own sinfulness will not make you less holy. It will not make you soft on sin. Rather, it will make you more likely to cast yourself on the Savior, to save you and to sanctify you. It will help you deal with your struggles according to the principles of Romans 6 and 8.

Admitting your struggle will also make you more believable in the world. Non-Christians are turned off by super-spiritual saints with their smug cliches, condescending smiles, and contradictory life-styles. Hypocrites don't easily win people to Christ.

And overexpecters who do not become hypocrites must necessarily become dropouts. Failing to reach the heights they expected, they just simply quit. Why bother to pursue the Christian life if the total victory is not won quickly?

This is a major reason why Christian baby boomers in increasing numbers have joined their disillusioned friends in the world and taken their own lives. Suicide sometimes seems the best way out when their guilt and despair are so great!

Dave was one such baby boomer. He took his own life one night in a Bible college dorm room. Shortly after an evening chapel service, he sought out two or three of his closest friends and told them good-bye. They curiously watched him walk alone toward his room. No one thought to follow and ask why he said "good-bye" instead of "good night." Dave was somewhat of a loner and often disappeared suddenly from campus activities.

An hour later they found his lifeless body next to the gun which had ended his frustrating struggle. A note told the tragic story.

At fourteen Dave had been sexually molested by a male youth sponsor in his church. The incident sparked a six-year struggle with homosexual desire which, until recently, had been effectively suppressed.

The molestation by the youth sponsor was a one-time affair, and neither Dave nor the sponsor ever mentioned it again. Thus Dave's life appeared to progress normally through his senior high years except for an embarrassing and distracting fantasy life. He often dreamed of homosexual encounters, an activity which heightened both his illicit desires and his sense of moral guilt and shame.

At seventeen Dave felt "called to preach" and rededicated himself to God and His plan for Dave's life. Those were spiritually and emotionally refreshing days, and for awhile it looked as though Dave's struggle with homosexuality had ended.

Then came Bible college with its typical freshman year stress. Dave tried hard to balance work, friends, and school amid a new and lonely environment. It was a very emotionally vulnerable time for Dave. College freshmen take their lives more frequently than any other group in our society.

To make a long and sordid story short, Dave once again became addicted to homosexual fantasies. This time they were accompanied by books and movies not available in Dave's hometown but easily accessible in the city. Dave knew he had to do something. He considered seeing a counselor. He knew he could not continue to live a lie. He also thought about suicide, especially during his most guilt-ridden hours, those immediately following his failures. It was during one of these times that he bought a gun.

Then came the night of the chapel service. The college had a special speaker that night, an evangelist known for his bold stand against sin in American society. His message was entitled "Homosexuality, America's Most Shameful Sin."

In his sermon the evangelist noted, that contrary to some liberals' opinions, "no one with homosexual tendencies was or could be a Christian." He based his view on 1 Corinthians 6:9-10 which reads in part, "Do not be deceived, homosexuals shall not inherit the kingdom of God." The evangelist did not mention that the covetous and cheaters were also grouped with homosexuals in that passage. Neither did he read verse eleven which affirms the possibility of total forgiveness even for homosexuals. The verse also admits the presence of such people (forgiven homosexuals) in the church at Corinth.

The evangelist said that homosexuality was a sin wherein "God gave men over to degrading passion." His point was that homosexuals had "no hope for recovery." They had chosen a life-style which made repentance not only unlikely but impossible.

So there it was—the speaker had justified Dave's thoughts of suicide. What other option was there for one with no hope for future recovery and no forgiveness for the past. Dave himself pulled the trigger, but, in effect, the overexpecting and biblically ignorant evangelist had loaded the gun.

The truth is that homosexual sin, like heterosexual sin, is both shameful and addicting. It is not, however, unpardonable nor unalterable. Dave already knew the former truth. He desperately needed to know the latter.

Unlike Dave, other overexpecting Christians don't kill their bodies. Instead, they kill their hope. They just give up on the whole Christian scene. They no longer make any effort to try to live for God. They don't believe all that religious stuff anymore. They become cynical and hardened. They are classic examples of how overexpecting will ultimately lead to underexpecting.

This is why God is so careful to point out the very real struggles of even His most choice servants. They motivate us to keep trying.

> Elijah was a man with a nature like ours, and he prayed earnestly that it might not rain; and it did not rain on the earth for three years and six months. And he prayed again, and the sky poured rain, and the earth produced its fruit (James 5:17-18).

Elijah was a man not so different from us. He had real struggles, yet his prayer mattered. God answered. God fought for him in spite of his struggle. And He will for us too.

So Romans 7 gives us both understanding and hope. We need only one more thing to help motivate us to keep faithful in spite of our struggle. We who struggle wrestle daily with self-hate. Our wretchedness has left us with intense guilt. So we need forgiveness.

Thus Romans 8 begins with a clear and consoling affirmation: "There is therefore now no condemnation for those who are in Christ Jesus" (Rom. 8:1). If we are in Christ, if we have believed on Him as our sin-bearing Savior, if we have repented of our sins, we are no longer condemned. Verse three says that He, by His death, condemned our sin, not us.

So in chapter 8 Paul asks the question: "Who will bring a charge against God's elect?" (Rom. 8:33). It is a rhetorical question with a qualitative pronoun. Paul is asking who—that is, what kind of person—has a right to accuse us? Jesus answered such a question with His remarks to the accusers of a woman caught in adultery. "He who is without sin among you, let him be the first to throw a stone at her" (John 8:7). Only the sinless have an undisputed and perfect right to accuse. And who are the sinless?

There is only one who is sinless. And so Paul answers his own question: "Who will bring a charge against God's elect? God is the one who justifies" (Rom. 8:33). Only God has a legal right to accuse, and He is not accusing us but justifying us. He has declared us righteous in His Son.

Paul continues the rhetorical questioning in verse 34.

> Who is the one who condemns? Christ Jesus is He who died, yes, rather who was raised, who is at the right hand of God, who also intercedes for us (Rom. 8:34).

Condemnation is more than just accusation. It is the next step in the judicial process. Condemnation presupposes the ability to carry out judgment. We can only be legally and effectively condemned by those who have both the authority and the power to execute the justice due us, to carry out our sentence.

So who can carry out the sentence our sin deserves? Who can send us to hell? Again there is only one who qualifies, and He died in our place. He rose again to prove our justification. He doesn't condemn us. He sits at the right hand of the Father and prays for us.

And these words are written to the believer. Jesus did not die only for the sins we committed as non-Christians. He died for all our sins—past, present, and future. His blood "continually cleanses us from all sin" (1 John 1:7). In Him we are totally forgiven.

Overexpecters need these words. When we expect quick and easy changes in our lives, we tend to be very hard on ourselves when we don't get them. But self-accusation, self-hate, and self-punishment will not atone for our sins. Neither will these attitudes free us from our sins. They will not make us better people.

The best climate for change is one of acceptance, not condemnation. Practical righteousness, according to Paul, comes to those who have their minds set on the Spirit (see Romans 8:4-6). And the mind of the Spirit in Romans 8 is one of forgiveness.

## THE LAW IN THE LIFE OF THE BELIEVER
*1 Timothy 1:8-9*

WHAT IT CAN DO

1. Expose sin
   *Romans 3:20; 7:7, 13*

2. Make sin increase
   *Romans 5:20; 7:5*
   *1 Corinthians 15:56*
   *Romans 7:8*

3. Show the need of a Savior
   *Galatians 3:24*

4. Lead to death
   *2 Corinthians 3:6-7*
   *Romans 7:9-11*

5. Condemn to punishment
   *2 Corinthians 3:9*
   *Deuteronomy 27:26*
   *James 2:10-11*
   *Galatians 3:10*

6. Produce self-righteousness
   *Philippians 3:9*

7. Lead to spiritual slavery
   *Romans 6:16; 7:5, 15, 24*

WHAT IT CANNOT DO

1. Depose sin
   *Romans 6:14*

2. Make sin decrease
   *Galatians 3:1-6*

3. Save
   *Romans 8:3*

4. Impart life
   *Galatians 3:21*

5. Declare righteous before God
   *Romans 3:20*
   *Galatians 2:16*

6. Produce real righteousness
   *Galatians 3:1-6*
   *Philippians 3:9*

7. Give spiritual freedom
   *Galatians 5:1; 2:19*
   *Romans 7:1-5; 6:14*

God, even when He disciplines us, is for us. He is on our side. He is not accusing but justifying us. He is not condemning but interceding for us. No wonder Paul concludes the chapter with such stirring words. They are the thoughts of a struggling Christian who has found in God understanding, hope, and forgiveness. They are words we baby boom believers need to read again with renewed gratefulness and hope.

> Who shall separate us from the love of Christ? Shall tribulation, or distress, or persecution, or famine, or nakedness, or peril, or sword?

Just as it is written, "For Thy sake we are being put to death all day long; we were considered as sheep to be slaughtered." But in all these things we overwhelmingly conquer through Him who loved us. For I am convinced that neither death, nor life, nor angels, nor principalities, nor things present, nor things to come, nor powers, nor height, nor depth, nor any other created thing, shall be able to separate us from the love of God, which is in Christ Jesus our Lord (Rom. 8:35-39).

# CHAPTER
# 6

## How Much Is Enough: Changing How We View Success

How do baby boomers view success? How much success is enough? To one California yuppie who told *Newsweek* she normally buys two outfits a week, enough is $200,000 a year—until she has children.[1] The example may be extreme, but it illustrates a common mind-set among baby boomers. For us baby boomers, enough—be it money, prestige, leisure time, or productive ministry—is always just a little bit more than what we now have.

Gordon MacDonald, in his book *Ordering Your Private World*,[2] agrees with the Datsun ad of the eighties—"We are driven!" Madison Avenue has raised our expectations to unscalable heights, our upbringing has filled us with impossible dreams, and, as a result, few of us feel successful. We rush around trying to be successful, but few of us are, at least in our own eyes. Few are satisfied, fulfilled, content with life. Most of us are restless, bored, and unproductive.

Our problem is that we have viewed success wrongly. We have set unrealistic and unbiblical goals which have left us both disillusioned and defeated. What we need is a new measuring stick. What is the biblical criteria for success? How much does God say is enough?

## NOT HOW MUCH BUT HOW FAITHFUL

In Scripture, God's measure of success is not quantitative but qualitative. In Matthew 25 Jesus tells the story of a man who goes on a journey entrusting each of three slaves with some of his money to invest in his absence. To the first he gave five talents (about four hundred pounds) of silver; to the second, two talents; and to the third, one talent.

After a long absence he returns and receives an accounting. The first two slaves had each doubled his money. The first now had ten talents; the second, four. Jesus commended each of them with the same words.

> Well done, good and faithful slave; you were faithful with a few things, I will put you in charge of many things; enter into the joy of your master (Matt. 25:23).

To Jesus the success of these slaves was not determined by how much they were given, but by how faithful they were in managing it. The concept is a consistent teaching in Scripture. God chooses people for ministry and then evaluates and rewards them, not on the basis of how much they have to work with, but how faithful they are with what they have (see 1 Cor. 4:1; 1 Tim. 1:12; 2 Tim. 2:2).

So how much is enough in God's eyes? Enough to God is faithful management—not of what you don't have but hope to someday—but of what you do have now, today.

The third slave in Jesus' story was probably an overexpecter. Instead of investing his one talent, he hid it until his master's return. Overexpecters are like that. They are rarely faithful in little things. Instead they wait for much, and then they plan to do great things for God and others.

"Just wait until I get that promotion," we say. "Or just wait until I receive my inheritance. Or maybe I'll win the *Reader's Digest* Sweepstakes or get a visit from Ed McMahon. Then I will start giving to God's work, or then I'll start saving for my retirement, or then I'll stop misusing credit."

The mind-set includes more than just our view of money. "Just wait until I get that new job," we say, "then I'll spend more time with the family, then I'll complete that important project, then I'll have more time for others."

*But enough is never enough for an overexpecter.* And when the income rises or the new job starts, we always need just a little more to start being faithful. The words of the master to the slave who hid the talent are a solemn warning to us.

> You wicked, lazy slave, you knew that I reap where I did not sow, and gather where I scattered no seed.
>
> Then you ought to have put my money in the bank, and on my arrival I would have received my money back with interest.
>
> Therefore take away the talent from him, and give it to the one who has the ten talents.
>
> For to everyone who has shall more be given, and he shall have an abundance; but from the one who does not have, even what he does have shall be taken away (Matt. 25:26-29).

Gordon MacDonald says that driven people are caught in an uncontrolled pursuit of expansion.[3] We baby boomers tend to define success too quantitatively. Bigger, we think, is always better. We need to read again the words of Zechariah: "Who has despised the day of small things?" (Zech. 4:10). We, not God, despise small things. We think they are unimportant, unworthy of our attention. God thinks they are most important. Indeed, He chooses them as the basis for our future reward!

Driven people also, says MacDonald, are highly competitive.[4] They not only want to be good at what they do, but better—in fact, best. But evaluating success on the basis of faithfulness eliminates such comparisons.

Paul said that those who compare themselves among themselves are unwise. Why? Because God does not compare us with one another. To do so would be like comparing snowflakes. There are no best snowflakes, only different ones, each beautiful in its own way. In fact, the variety only serves to enhance their individual beauty. Each contributes to the attractiveness of the other.

So it is with the body of Christ. We are all different, yet these very differences contribute to the beauty of the whole. I help your attractiveness by being me, not by trying to be you. God does not want us to be clones of one another. While we do well to imitate the good qualities we see in others, too much comparing can lead to frustration. Christ is our supreme model, not others. And we stand before Him not on the basis of how we stack up against others but how we stack up against ourselves. How faithful are we with the "talents" He has given us?

How about you? Are you measuring your success by how big your paycheck is when compared to that of a colleague? Or is success to you a bigger house than your friends down the street? Or is it a church with more people than the others in town?

Such expectations will always be self-defeating. They will never leave us content. There is always someone bigger and better. And if you do become best in one area, you will not be so in others at the same time. And, most important, such quantitative expectations will divert our attention from the real issue, which is not how much we have, but how we manage it.

## NOT THE RESULT BUT THE PROCESS

Because God measures success in terms of faithfulness rather than size, then what we do today, with the little we do have, has much more bearing on our success than the future results of such labor. Or to put it another way, the process is more important than the future goal.

But baby boomers are driven people, and driven people, says MacDonald, are more occupied with results than with the process for obtaining those results.[5] We want to see the business flourish, the project completed, the church filled. And until we do, there will be no success, and no accompanying sense of fulfillment and contentment.

The apostle Paul, on the other hand, made the process his goal.

> I planted, Apollos watered, but God was causing the growth. So then neither the one who plants nor the one who waters is anything, but God who causes the growth. Now he who plants and he who waters are one; but each will receive his own reward according to his own labor (1 Cor. 3:6-8).

Paul measured his success in terms of faithful planting, not reaping. God would cause the growth in His time. The end result was up to Him.

We baby boomers need to do likewise. We will never be more successful someday with much than we are now with little. We need to focus more on the process than the end goal. We need to work hard today on our business, spend some time today on our unfinished project, work hard today on serving others, and God will cause the growth in His time.

And not only will we never be more successful someday with much than we are today with little, we will never be more satisfied and content with much someday, than we are today with little. If we can't enjoy the little, we'll never enjoy the much.

Thus you will probably not enjoy your kids when they are grown if you do not enjoy them as children. You will probably not be a content married person if you are not a content single. You will not be happy with $100,000 a year if you cannot be so on $10,000 a year. Enough is never enough when we overexpect.

And making the process our goal will also help us "slow down and smell the roses." Gordon MacDonald says that driven people not only focus on accomplishments rather than the process, they are also abnormally busy people.[6] While laziness is clearly frowned upon in the Bible (especially by the writer of Proverbs), it does not gives us role models who were obsessive workers. The men and women of Scripture did not measure their success by how many hours of work they could cram into one day. They knew that each day was a day the Lord had made, therefore they "rejoiced and were glad in it!" They enjoyed the process. Do you?

## NOT HOW WE START BUT HOW WE FINISH

A faithful man will abound
  with blessings,
But he who makes haste to be
  rich will not go unpunished
(Prov. 28:20).

We just looked at the way so many baby boomers are obsessively goal-oriented. Oddly enough, even with this goal fixation, overexpecters are usually long on starting things and short on finishing them. They want success now, not later. This is a natural outcome of goal fixation, for if the end result is everything, then the end cannot be postponed for long. The process must be shortened in any way possible. Thus overexpecting baby boomers fall easily for get-rich-quick schemes, crash diets, and quickie success seminars.

But wise King Solomon said that sprinting the first lap will usually end in an early retirement from the race. The key to winning is faithfulness—setting a pace and keeping with it.

In Matthew 25 Jesus tells a parable of ten young ladies who went out to greet the bridegroom in an ancient Hebrew wedding. They took with them oil-burning lamps. Those who brought extra oil were ready to meet their guest when he arrived unexpectedly late at midnight. The others missed out. They had not come prepared to stay for the long haul and were away buying more oil when the bridegroom came.

The point is clear: God wants us to not only begin well but to end well. We need to be marathon runners, not sprinters. There are no short cuts to our objectives. Success comes to those who faithfully persevere.

These are balancing words for those of us who believe in the pretribulational rapture of the church. Yes, Jesus may come today. We must be ready. He may also come a hundred years from today. We must be faithful until the end.

## NOT EASE BUT ENDURANCE

Success for most baby boomers is a life of ease, comfort, luxury, and undisturbed leisure. The life-styles of the rich and famous have taught us so. In fact, even the religious rich and famous— many of our Christian celebrities and superstars—seem to verify the concept that success and luxury go hand in hand.

Yet nothing could be further from the biblical reality. Periods of ease and comfort were the exception for most biblical characters, not the rule. Most lived tough lives in which pain and adversity were frequent companions.

And not only did the men and women of Scripture find pain a significant part of their experience, it was also a part of their theology. Suffering was included in the "all things" God works through to benefit those who love Him (see Rom. 8:28). Thus it is not to be avoided but endured.

> Consider it all joy, my brethren, when you encounter various trials, knowing that the testing of your faith produces endurance (James 1:2-3).

Since we baby boomers have been raised to view success as ease, most of us are not very good at enduring. When the boss is unreasonable, we quit. When the subjects are too difficult, we drop out. When marriage gets unbearable, we get a divorce.

Our great mobility has allowed us to get to places faster than ever before. It has also allowed us to leave faster. It has become easy to quit. No-fault divorce is a natural result of a society that likes to leave itself an easy out in almost everything.

We need to stop measuring success by how easy life is and start working on our endurance. Success is not freedom from pain. Success is hanging in there, even when it hurts.

It will help to get our eyes off those who seem to have it made in this life. The Bible teaches that their ease is as transient as summer grass under the late August sun. This world's success will fade and perish as quickly as it appeared in the first place. Instead we must focus on the reward that will last.

> Therefore we do not lose heart, but though our outer man is decaying, yet our inner man is being renewed day by day. For momentary, light affliction is producing for us an eternal weight of glory far beyond all comparison (2 Cor. 4:16-17).

## NOT WHO SERVES US BUT WHOM WE SERVE

Some of Jesus' disciples were probably overexpecters. They, like the typical overexpecter, tended to measure success quantitatively. For instance, success to them was gained by being the top man in the group, the leader, the one whom all the others would both follow and serve.

The problem was that they could not come to an agreement on who that person was among themselves. They often argued over who among them was the greatest. It was on the heels of such an argument that Jesus spoke these words:

You know that those who are recognized as rulers of the Gentiles lord it over them; and their great men exercise authority over them. But it is not so among you, but whoever wishes to become great among you shall be your servant; and whoever wishes to be first among you, shall be slave of all. For even the Son of Man did not come to be served, but to serve, and to give His life a ransom for many (Mark 10:42-45).

To Jesus success was not measured by who serves you, but by whom you serve. The top man in His book is not the one being served, but the one doing the serving.

Probably no single aspect of the baby boom mentality has done more to harm the cause of Christ than its self-centeredness, its emphasis on individual happiness and success. At the same time, probably no single aspect of our mentality has done more to rob us of the very things we seek. Happiness and success seem to come most readily to those who seek them least, to those who instead devote themselves to serving others.

By the way, in the area of serving our generation's size will work for us, not against us. While managerial positions are scarce due to generational crowding (there are plenty of bosses among us), opportunities to serve abound. And competition is low. This generation is not scrambling over one another to get a chance to serve.

## NOT WHAT WE ACCOMPLISH INDIVIDUALLY BUT AS A GROUP

The Corinthian church must have been filled with overexpecters. Paul chides no other church as much for self-centeredness and divisions in its ranks.

In chapter 12 he reminds them of something fundamental to

God's concept of success. In the church, the body of Christ, we are all on the same team, part of the same body.

> And if one member suffers, all the members suffer with it; if one member is honored, all the members rejoice with it (1 Cor. 12:26).

Paul says that we win or lose together in the body of Christ. His are not theoretical words. The church is like a body, and no one has ever yet won a race with his right hand while, at the same time, losing with his left foot. Body parts win or lose together, and so do members of the church.

Thus success, if it comes to baby boom believers, will come collectively or not at all. We must reject the narcissistic isolationism of the seventies and eighties and return to the sense of community of the late sixties. Again, our size will be our ally. We have never accomplished as separate individuals what we did as a unit. Witness the end to the war in Vietnam. With their frequent demonstrations, baby boomers—acting as a group—helped bring about the end of the war by influencing politicians and public opinion.

Thus we need to stop focusing attention so much on ourselves and our happiness, and dwell more on the success of those around us. We need to make it our goal to help them do well. Fellowship has never been optional for the church. It is especially important in our day. We need each other.

But succeeding together does not come easily for baby boomers. Our heroes were not usually team players. Superman could leap buildings in a single bound. He also captured the bad guys single-handedly. And if Jimmie Olson or Lois Lane tried to help, they only ended up in need of rescue themselves. We grew up thinking that heroes function best by themselves.

At the same time baby boomers at large were watching Superman, baby boomers in the church were reading Christian biographies and listening to sermons which seemed to suggest the same situation. We were told that the world has yet to see what God can do through the person who is totally yielded to Him. We wanted to someday be that person. We would someday single-handedly win a continent for Christ.

Yet biblical heroes did not usually win alone. King David slew Goliath as others watched, but he had his Joab and his mighty men for future battles. Elijah single-handedly slew four hundred prophets of Baal on Mount Carmel, but when he started complaining that he was all alone, God reminded him of seven thousand people still in Israel who had not bowed to the pagan deity.

The apostle Paul had his Timothy and Titus. And if the mostly unheralded Barnabas had not been around, Paul himself might have lived a life of obscurity.

The point is, we all need God *and others* to succeed in life. We will not save the world alone. The same goes for our marriages, our children, our businesses, and our churches.

## NOT HOW VISIBLE BUT HOW REAL

Have you noticed? Many if not most of God's servants have been developed in obscurity. Away from life's center stage, they endured long tedious hours in the remote and unheralded sectors of life.

For most of them a season of public success was only the tip of a very large iceberg. The great unseen mass of their days had been lived in obscurity. Here they were slowly, carefully, sometimes painfully molded by God.

So Abraham lived most of his life as an obscure desert nomad. Ditto for Isaac and Jacob.

Joseph became prime minister of Egypt, but not until he had spent thirteen long years unnoticed in the pits and dungeons of the land.

Moses grew up in a palace, then spent forty years tending sheep in the wilderness. Only then did God install him in a place of leadership.

David was anointed king as a young shepherd boy. Yet after a brief period of fame and honor, he spent the next several years hiding out in caves as he fled from the enraged Saul.

And obscurity is not unique to Old Testament saints. The apostle Paul did not begin his successful ministry immediately after meeting Jesus on the road to Damascus. First he spent two and one half years in the Arabian desert. Later he was thrown out of both Damascus and Jerusalem. He finally returned to his own hometown where he spent years in obscurity before Barnabas brought him to Antioch.

Outside of a select few, the majority of Jesus' disciples returned to obscurity after His death and resurrection. Men like Thomas, Nathaniel, and Andrew spent the majority of their days serving God outside the arena of public acclaim.

Jesus Himself spent most of His days in obscurity. The Son of God, the King of kings, was born not in a palace, but in a stable. He was not welcome company among Israel's elite. Most of His thirty-three years on this planet were not spent preaching or working miracles, but rather shaping wood in a carpenter's shop in one of Galilee's more remote villages. Yet it pleased the Father to raise His only Son in this way.

And so God still uses obscurity to develop us. It has a way of weaning us from the praise of men, from what Jesus called "practicing our righteousness before men to be noticed by them." Obscurity promotes genuineness. It tends to keep us honest. Certainly we saw, in the late eighties, evidence that celebrity Christians could come to practice deception in scandalous fashion. The limelight is not the best light for growing faithful believers. There is something to be said for being unknown.

And most of us baby boomers will get all the obscurity we can handle. Our generation's size alone will relegate us to a place of relative unimportance—unimportance in the world's eyes, at any rate. But being unheralded and unnoticed does not come easy for most of us—not when we were raised to expect both fortune and *fame*.

Perhaps it will help to remember that our present activities on this planet are not really obscure at all to the One who will one day eternally honor His own. His concern is not with our present visibility but our unseen genuineness. How real are we? How faithful are we in not only the little, but the unnoticed areas of life?

Canton, Ohio, is the home of pro football's Hall of Fame. They're all there—Doak Walker, Johnny Unitas, Vince Lombardi, Jim Brown, and a host of others. All excelled in their discipline, and, as a result, football history will never forget them.

We all have an innate desire to be remembered like that, to leave an indelible mark on this planet, to provide a positive testimony to future generations, to be enshrined in someone's hall of fame.

Yet, someday the Hall of Fame in Canton will crumble. And, like the ancient Roman gladiators who preceded them, names like Bart Starr and Roger Staubach will be forgotten. The things of this world are like that. They're temporal, transitory, subject to age and decay.

Not so with God's Hall of Fame. Hebrews 11 contains a partial listing of men and women

> who by faith conquered kingdoms, performed acts of righteousness, obtained promises, shut the mouths of lions, quenched the power of fire, escaped the edge of the sword, from weakness were made strong, became mighty in war, and put foreign armies to flight (Heb. 11:33-34).

Names like Enoch, Abraham, Joseph, and Moses will never be forgotten. They have been enshrined permanently in the visible memory of the God of Eternity.

Do you sometimes feel overlooked and unnoticed by men? Remember "God is not unjust so as to forget your work and the love which you have shown toward His name" (Heb. 6:10).

God's Hall of Fame included not only those the world noticed, but those it did not. In fact, it includes those the world abused and persecuted.

> And others experienced mockings and scourgings, yes, also chains and imprisonment. They were stoned, they were sawn in two, they were tempted, they were put to death with the sword; they went about in sheepskins, in goatskins, being destitute, afflicted, ill-treated (men of whom the world was not worthy), wandering in the deserts and mountains and caves and holes in the ground (Heb. 11:36-38).

Thus, this life may well end without adequate recognition, but the one to come will begin with it. Your God who sees in private will someday reward you in public. So hang in there. God is watching your game films. And His Hall of Fame is still open for new additions.

## NOT HOW ASSERTIVE BUT HOW MEEK

"Blessed are the meek," said Jesus, "for they will inherit the earth."

What radical words, in His day and ours! Browse through the self-help section of any bookstore in our land and peruse the titles. Baby boomers obviously don't believe the spoils go to the meek. Rather, self-assertion is the way to get ahead in life. One needs to learn the art of "creative aggression." You must "look out for Number One," and "pull your own strings."

But such an attitude is the exact opposite of meekness. It is diametrically and fundamentally opposed. That's why we baby boomers are "driven." Gordon MacDonald says that the driven often sacrifice their integrity to get ahead in life.[7] We have bought the world's view that assertiveness brings success. We need to learn again the biblical concept of meekness.

Meekness in the Bible is defined mostly by example. Discover the biblical characters who were meek and you will learn the meaning of the term. Abraham was such a man. Perhaps we see his meekness best in Genesis 13 when his employees quarrel with the employees of his nephew, Lot.

Abraham and Lot both have large flocks of sheep. Thus they can no longer graze them together. They must split up and occupy different parts of the land of Canaan. Abraham's words to Lot show his meekness.

> Then Abram said to Lot, "Please let there be no strife between you and me, nor between my herdsmen and your herdsmen, for we are brothers. Is not the whole land before you? Please separate from me: if to the left, then I will go to the right; or if to the right, then I will go to the left" (Gen. 13:8-9).

Abraham had been promised the land by God. It was his by right, all of it. He had every right to choose the best for himself. Yet for the sake of unity in his family, he did not pull his own strings.

By the way, Abraham was not a weak man. In the very next chapter of Genesis he goes to war against men who are oppressing the innocent. Meekness is often righteously aggressive. But it is never selfishly assertive.

Lot, on the other hand, was a driven man, and he did exactly as you would expect a driven man to do. He chose the best land for himself.

They had to wait twenty-five years, one quarter of a century, to see the fruit of their decisions. Lot seemed to prosper in the short run, but lost it all in the end. Abraham, on the other hand, really did "inherit the land."

Meek people are willing to wait on God. They will not compromise important things for instant gratification. They see the "Lots" in this world making it by selfish self-assertion, but they know their success is, at best, short-lived. They have taken the advice of the psalmist and are letting God pull their strings.

Do not fret because of evildoers,
    Be not envious toward wrongdoers.
For they will wither quickly like the grass,
    And fade like the green herb.
Trust in the LORD, and do good;
    Dwell in the land and cultivate faithfulness.
Delight yourself in the LORD;
    and He will give you the desires of your heart
(Ps. 37:1-4).

The meek do not have a psychology of entitlement. They know the difference between rights and privileges. They have learned from Jesus' parable in Luke 17.

But which of you, having a slave plowing or tending sheep, will say to him when he has come in from the field, "Come immediately and sit down to eat?" But will he not say to him, "Prepare something for me to eat, and *properly* clothe yourself and serve me until I have eaten and drunk; and afterward you will eat and drink"? He does not thank the slave because he did the things which were commanded, does he? So you too, when you do all the things which are commanded you, say, "We are unworthy slaves; we have done *only* that which we ought to have done" (Luke 17:7-10).

Jesus says, in effect, don't confuse the rights of a slave with those of a master. God is master. We are slaves. He deserves to be waited on first. We do not. He then assumes ultimate responsibility for our basic needs. We do not.

The mind-set, if we adapt it, will breed both gratefulness and peace. Every time we receive more than our basic needs we realize that these are privileges, not rights. These privileges may include the fact that we live in a free country and thus are able to prosper from our own initiative and hard work, but make no mistake, they are still privileges. They are blessings we as mere slaves do not deserve, but which God as a good Master has freely and graciously given. And if we seem to lack basic needs, we don't get overly anxious. Instead we remember our Master's reassuring words to His disciples.

> And do not seek what you shall eat, and what you shall drink, and do not keep worrying. For all these things the nations of the world eagerly seek; but your Father knows that you need these things. But seek for His kingdom, and these things shall be added to you (Luke 12:29-31).

And, the meek are not resentful toward those who have more than they do. It is the Master's right to distribute the talents as He wishes. We can all think of people who seem to have more than us but, in our opinion, deserve it less. But we can also, if we are honest, think of those who have less but deserve it more. In fact, if we live in America, these are by far the more numerous. In 1987, 2.3 billion people, nearly half the population of the world, existed on an income of roughly one U.S. dollar a day. If life is unfair, we are the better for it.

And we have dealt with only economic gratefulness. What about spiritual blessing? Do we have reason to be grateful in this area?

Do you remember the Vietnamese boat people, those refugees who escaped their homeland with literally only the shirts on their backs? Spiritually speaking, the Bible teaches we are all boat people. The apostle Paul says we Gentile Christians should "remember that you were separate from Christ, excluded from the commonwealth of Israel, and strangers to the covenants of promise, having no hope and without God in the world" (Eph. 2:12).

Before Christ died for us and drew us to Himself, we were as spiritually bankrupt as those Vietnamese boat people. We had no spiritual homeland and no possessions. We were without hope. We had no promise of a better future, no savior to rescue us from our sinking ship. Our sins had condemned us to a Christless eternity in hell.

Yet God who is rich in mercy and love not only saved us from hell but gave us "every spiritual blessing in the heavenly places" (Eph. 1:3).

So we baby boomers need a new attitude toward God and His blessing. We need to start wisely managing, generously sharing, and gratefully enjoying what we do have, rather than longing for and resenting those who possess what we do not. We already have far more than we deserve.

Finally, meek people are not harried and always uptight. They are not collapsing beneath a self-imposed load of unrealistic and unbiblical expectations. They have accepted the invitation of their Master:

> Come to Me, all who are weary and heavy-laden, and I will give you rest. Take My yoke upon you, and learn from Me, for I am gentle and humble in heart; and you shall find rest for your souls. For My yoke is easy, and my load is light (Matt. 11:28-30).

No burden is so heavy as the one we place on ourselves by our overexpectations. It is a burden which has made us driven, and then very, very tired. Jesus says it is a burden we no longer have to carry. It is a burden we need to give to Him.

By the way, drivenness not only makes us uptight and tired, it often does not work, either.

Unless the LORD builds the house,
They labor in vain who build it;
Unless the LORD guards the city,
The watchman keeps awake in vain.
It is vain for you to rise up early,
To retire late,
To eat the bread of painful labors;
For He gives to His beloved even in his sleep
(Ps. 127:1-2).

The self-assertive person forgets that self effort has its limits. Even hard work, though good, may be futile. Driven people end up in a position of trying to play God. They must themselves produce what only God can ultimately guarantee, real growth and security. Often they build and watch in vain.

On the other hand, the meek person need not become a workaholic. Hard work is good, but overwork is unnecessary. God gives to the meek even as they sleep.

We baby boomers really have become our own worst enemies. Other generations have endured harsher economic and political times. The church has survived greater persecution and more decadent societies. Many saints who lived in tougher days were more content, joyful, and productive than we. Our problem is not our tough circumstances. It is our own unfulfillable expectations. And we can do something about them. We can take seriously Jesus' invitation. We can lay our expectations at His feet.

Are you tired of chasing pretty rainbows?
Are you tired of spinning round and round?
Wrap up all the shattered dreams of your life,
And at the feet of Jesus lay them down.

Give them all, give them all, give them all to Jesus.
Shattered dreams, wounded hearts, broken toys.

Give them all, give them all, give them all to Jesus.
And He will turn your sorrow into joy.

He never said you'd only see sunshine.
He never said there'd be no rain.
He only promised us a heart full of singing,
At the very thing that once brought pain.

Give them all, give them all, give them all to Jesus.
Shattered dreams, wounded hearts, broken toys.
Give them all, give them all, give them all to Jesus.
And He will turn your sorrow into joy.[8]

# CHAPTER

# 7

# *Murphy's Law and the Fall: Balancing Our Expectations*

"If anything can go wrong, it will." You are acquainted with Murphy's Law, but have you read the corollaries?

"Nothing is as easy as it looks."

"Everything takes longer than you think."

"If you perceive that there are four possible ways in which a procedure can go wrong and circumvent these, then a fifth way will promptly develop."

"Every solution breeds new problems."

"It is impossible to make anything foolproof because fools are so ingenious."

Ever wondered how Murphy's Law got started? When did nature start siding with the hidden flaw? Genesis 3 tells us.

The first man, Adam, acting as the representative head of all of us who follow him (see Romans 5), sinned against God. Thus God drove him and his wife, Eve, from the sinless paradise called Eden to a place cursed because of their sin.

Theologians call this the Fall. We live in a fallen world. The concept has great importance for our expectations. Things are not perfect in the world—not our bodies, our souls, our relationships, our jobs, our governments, our churches. All creation is fallen, a condition which causes us great agony. The Bible says it makes us "groan within ourselves" (Rom. 8:23).

But Genesis 3 also contains a promise. The seed of the woman would someday "bruise the head of the serpent," a promise most Bible scholars believe is messianic, that is, a prophecy of the coming Messiah.

There would be a second Adam, a man who by His one act of righteousness would offer justification to all men. The man was Jesus, the God-man.

And the Bible teaches that not only would Christ die to redeem mankind, He would come again, a second time, to redeem all creation (see Romans 8:19-21). There is coming a day when the effects of the Fall will be lifted from the earth. There will be no more pain, no more tears, no more death; and thank God, no more Professor Murphy and his horrible laws.

Until such a time we have two major responsibilities. One, we are to fight against the effects of the Fall. Two, we are to learn to be content even in a fallen world.

The command given to man in Genesis 1 to subdue and rule over creation remained in effect after the Fall. It is still a responsibility of mankind. In fact, it is even more important in a fallen world. Thus man tries to find cures for diseases, new techniques to increase agricultural productivity, and new ways to develop and harness the world's energy.

Such activity has a firm base in Christian thought. It differs radically from the increasingly popular New Age view, which sees nature as basically good. (Having no transcendent God to speak of, New Age proponents often give a high place in their thought to nature, which is usually portrayed as being completely benevolent. Most actually identify God with nature.) New Agers urge us to accept and cooperate with nature rather than fight her. But fallen nature dare not be let alone. It is too destructive. Man must rule over the earth.

We also try to deal with the effects of the Fall on the spiritual and moral levels. Thus we try to feed the hungry, promote just laws in government, and win people to Christ. These things will not just naturally happen on their own. Not in a fallen world. We must work for them.

However, to function in a fallen world, we must also learn contentment. The apostle Paul's words illustrate the concept of contentment in a fallen world.

> Not that I speak from want; for I have learned to be content in whatever circumstances I am.
>
> I know how to get along with humble means, and I also know how to live in prosperity; in any and every circumstance I have learned the secret of being filled and going hungry, both of having abundance and suffering need. I can do all things through Him who strengthens me (Phil. 4:11-13).

Poverty is a result of the Fall. No one will go hungry in the new heavens and new earth. Thus poverty is one of those things we should fight against until the Lord returns.

Yet Paul did not fight poverty at every level and at every opportunity. At least, he did not fight hard against his own lack. At times, when he went hungry, he learned to be content. He lowered his expectations in this area. He was temporarily satisfied with what he did have rather than longing for what he did not have.

Why did Paul do so? Because in a fallen world contentment is necessary. Nothing will ever be perfect in this life. If we try to work until it is, we will literally work ourselves to death. Or we will work exclusively in one area and never address other important issues in life. (If a person labored all his life to alleviate material poverty, for example, he would probably do so at the neglect of spiritual poverty.) Or, more likely, we will simply give up. Remember, most underexpecters are really frustrated overexpecters. If we can't have the whole pie, we do not even want a slice. This is both a childish and self-defeating attitude to say the least.

Thus we are to both fight the effects of the Fall and be content in a fallen world. They are balancing tensions. If we are too content with some aspects of the Fall—if we just accept this world as it is and do not try to change it—we lose our saltiness as Christians. We conform to rather than impact our world. We exercise complacency, not contentment.

So how do we find contentment in a fallen world? How do we, at the same time, vigorously fight the effects of the Fall?

## BATTLEGROUND LIVING

We do so, first of all, by not expecting too much from the world. Not only does the Bible teach that this world is fallen, it also teaches it is at war with its Creator and His servants. Jesus said that we should expect tribulation. Paul taught that we wrestle against not mere flesh and blood but powerful spiritual entities. Life is not a rose garden. It is a battleground.

This sounds too painful to think about for long, and many people, even many Christians, fail to come to grips with the world's fallenness. Yet such a bleak perspective will actually help us find contentment in life. C. S. Lewis put it this way:

> If you think of this world as a place intended simply for our happiness, you find it quite intolerable: think of it as a place of training and correction and it's not so bad.
>
> Imagine a set of people all living in the same building. Half of them think it is a hotel, the other half think it is a prison. Those who think it a hotel might regard it as quite intolerable, and those who thought it was a prison might decide that it was really surprisingly comfortable. So that what seems the ugly doctrine is one that comforts and strengthens

you in the end. The people who try to hold an optimistic view of this world would become pessimists: the people who hold a pretty stern view of it become optimistic.[1]

We baby boomers were raised expecting to live our days in a posh hotel. In fact, many of us lived in something close during the affluent fifties and sixties. (A popular song from the seventies told us, "You don't know what you've got till it's gone," and how true that is.) Thus we have been disillusioned and pessimistic in the seventies and eighties. Our hotel has become our prison.

We need to regain the biblical view of the world as a battleground. Tragedy will hurt us, but it should not shock us. It is the stuff one finds in war. At the same time our battleground is not filled with only tragedy. Sometimes there is victory. Often there is rest. There are joys. These can be thoroughly and unashamedly enjoyed, but only if we see them as the exception rather than the rule. We can be content only when we don't expect too much.

We baby boomers have expected far too much from this life and far too little from the one to come. We've heard too many sermons on the abundant life and too few on heaven and the final redemption of God's people. An older generation of Christians may have overemphasized the life of the world to come, but that has not been true of our generation. We are not so heavenly minded that we are no earthly good. Rather, we are so earthly minded that we have little time for heavenly good.

The truth is that this life is not always that abundant, not even for a Christian, not even for a mature Christian. The success gospel has taught us that Christianity is always a good deal—in the next world, but, more important, in *this* one. The temporal payoffs, like increased prosperity, health, peace, and popularity, are always worth the effort of living for God. So we are told.

But the apostle Paul disagreed. "If we have hoped in Christ in this life only, we are of all men most to be pitied" (1 Cor. 15:19). There are, to be sure, blessings in life. There are also great tragedies.

Good people sometimes suffer immeasurably. They lose their jobs, mates, and children. They come down with debilitating diseases. They die early.

In a fallen world the innocent often get punished while the guilty escape. The righteous flounder while the wicked prosper. Good guys often lose and bad ones often win. If this world and time is all there is, then Christianity might not be such a good deal after all. In fact, we might as well consider becoming existential hedonists, living purely for pleasure. The apostle Paul knew this was the logical consequence of having no eternal hope: "If the dead are not raised, let us eat and drink, for tomorrow we die" (1 Cor. 15:32).

But the dead *are* raised. Christ's resurrection proved that. He is coming again to redeem fallen creation and fallen but saved man, including you and me. And when He does, He will also reward our faithfulness, faithfulness which has often been painfully lived out in a fallen world. Then, and only then, will it be worth it all.

In chapter 2 I mentioned Tom and Kay, the disillusioned couple who lost their only child. Tom and Kay need to remember that they live in a fallen world. God did not bring death into the world—not directly, anyway. Sin did. Man did (see Rom. 5:12). God did not let Tom and Kay down. Their expectations did. This fallen world did.

Jesus wept at the funeral of His friend, Lazarus. Tom and Kay's feelings of anger and grief are not opposed but shared by the One who can "sympathize with our weaknesses." Jesus walked where we walk. He felt this world's pain firsthand. He died so that it might one day end. He died so that Tom and Kay's daughter Sherry might be resurrected some day in a body that will no longer be subject to death. This is the hope that can sustain Tom and Kay in their grief. This is the hope that will sustain you and me in similar tragedies.

## SEVERE WEATHER BENEVOLENCE

If you live in west Texas, where late spring and early summer thunderheads often top fifty thousand feet, then you know what real storm clouds look like. You've seen firsthand those dark and billowing perpetrators of destruction. You may even have felt the sudden terror caused by a funnel cloud dipping unexpectedly and moving in your direction.

It is a feeling not unlike that experienced by baby boomers as we see the ominous storm clouds of our day. Harsh economic times are indeed threatening, but they seem like nothing compared with the threat of global nuclear war, or nuclear accidents, or nuclear weapons in the hands of terrorists, or the seemingly unstoppable AIDS epidemic. Face it, we live in scary days.

So how do we cope with times like these? How do we find courage to live on the battleground? The answer comes in realizing that not only should we not expect too much from this fallen world, we should, at the same time, not expect too little from our sovereign and omnipotent God.

The Bible teaches that God exercises a kind of severe weather benevolence. Meaning, He seems to do His best work in the shadow of some rather ominous clouds of doom.

Like sending Moses to liberate His people from the dark clouds of Egyptian oppression.

Or leading the young shepherd David to deliver Israel from a giant cloud of Philistine intimidation.

Or sustaining Elijah in the midst of suffocating clouds of national idolatry.

Or the Son of God Himself, sent to earth to die for our sins while dark clouds seemed to try to hide from heaven itself the ultimate atrocity of man.

In all these cases, the storm clouds were not only a sign of impending doom, they were an occasion for divine benevolence. They provided God with a unique opportunity to do what He

119

does best, to bring good from evil, joy from sorrow, life from death.

Such knowledge will help us cope with the days ahead. Storm clouds may be great, but the One who stilled the storm with a single word is still greater. And He continues to exercise severe weather benevolence on behalf of His own.

## WHEN LITTLE IS PLENTY

Yes, living in a fallen world requires some special attitudes. It will help to view life as a battleground, to not expect too much from this world. It will help to remember the principle of severe weather benevolence, to not expect too little from God. And it will help to know that with God our little is plenty. We need to avoid expecting too little from the little we have to offer Him.

The story of the feeding of the five thousand illustrates the concept. The need was great and the resources were low. Five thousand men, plus women and children, desperately needed a meal. Yet the only food on hand was the sack lunch of one young boy, just a couple of small fish and five biscuits.

Jesus taught a profound principle that day. With Him, our little is always plenty. Five thousand full stomachs and twelve baskets of leftovers underlined the lesson. Not only does being faithful in little make sense in eternity, it often makes sense in time. Not only will it bring reward someday, it will often bring results today.

Let me illustrate the concept with a problem common to many of us: dieting. Doctors and researchers are unanimous in their conclusions. Most people who successfully lose weight do so a little at a time. In fact, it is their consistency in little that helps them make the necessary changes in life-style that sustain their weight loss over a long period of time.

On the other hand, crash diets and other radical, quickie measures for losing weight do not have a good record of success.

Instead, they tend to promote a hopeless cycle of binging and abstaining which usually ends in more frustration and more obesity.

The problem is that most people who have chronic weight problems are overexpecters. Often they want to lose pounds much more than their friends who succeed in doing so. Their very expectations are what consistently defeat them.

One day they look in the mirror and decide they have had enough of being overweight. They will no longer tolerate the problem. Today they will absolutely not eat. Their expectations are dramatic. "I must lose ten pounds this week."

But crash diets don't often work. Neither do get-rich-quick schemes, or unrealistic exercise programs. In fact, even most so-called spiritual changes will not come all at once. Someone who is not spending a regular daily time in prayer and Bible reading will not often succeed with a plan to begin doing so for one full hour a day.

Two notes of warning need to be sounded here. One, the dieting illustration, though valid, is also somewhat simplistic. People vary greatly in regard to weight problems. Those who have been consistently unsuccessful in losing weight probably need to see both a medical doctor and a good biblical counselor. Then, with this added perspective, they can apply the principle of being faithful in little.

Two, we need to differentiate between overeating and other addictive behaviors like alcoholism or sexual promiscuity. To break addictions, most authorities, and Scripture itself, suggest going cold turkey, practicing total abstinence. Thus being faithful in little for the alcoholic does not mean only one or two drinks a day. Rather, it means being faithful only for today, living without alcohol one day at a time. Overexpecting would, in this instance, mean looking at the long span of one's lifetime and saying, "I will never, never drink again." But God gives grace to resist evil *today*, not tomorrow. "Do not be anxious for tomorrow; for tomorrow will care for itself. Each day has enough trouble of its own" (Matt. 6:34).

So you see, God does not ask for what we do not have, only what we do. Like the young man with the sack lunch, we offer Him our little amount of resolve, our little talents, our little courage, our little time; and He takes it from there. With God a little is always plenty!

## BALANCING YOUR EXPECTATIONS

The remainder of this chapter will provide you a format for balancing your own expectations. It will give you a chance to think through a number of important areas and examine these expectations. You can decide if you expect too much, too little, or both (which is usually the case). And, if so, you can then decide what to do about it.

For best results, do this exercise alone the first time. Then go over it with a close friend. They may help you to see things you did not notice at first. In the case of addictive behavior it might also be a good idea to seek the help of a trained biblical counselor. Many of these behaviors are escapist activities and may be the result of still other unfulfilled expectations.

Perhaps a personal illustration will help you get started. At one time I had great expectations for additional graduate education. I wanted to receive both a masters and a doctorate in my area of study.

But my expectations did not fit my reality. Because of family and ministry obligations, it was not realistic to become a full-time resident student in a seminary. I tried to do so twice, but each time economic realities forced me to drop out.

Finally, my expectation bust was too great, and I gave up. I became an underexpecter. I developed and implemented no goals for continuing education.

Then I discovered the biblical principle of being faithful in little. I identified with the slave who hid his talent. I decided it was expecting too little to have no plan for continuing education (no plan other than my frustrated plan for full-time seminary, that is). After all, the Bible teaches that the pursuit of wisdom is to be a lifetime endeavor.

So I decided there were things I could do. I could try to read widely and consistently. I could look into extension and correspondence courses. I could get private tutoring to help with areas of difficulty.

Thus I went from expecting too much, to expecting too little, to developing a plan for being faithful in little. So this is my new plan. No, it isn't what I originally wanted. But the alternate plan is working fairly well. I am learning to faithfully use the time and funds I have to continue my education. It is my prayer that you too will be able to adjust your expectations in the exercises that follow.

As you do, you will need to deal with both kinds of overexpectations. On the one hand, you may overexpect because of specific unbiblical expectations. On the other hand, you may expect too much because you are not adequately dealing with the Fall in general. Expecting God to always provide you with a new car would be an example of the first type of overexpectation. Expecting your present car to never wear out would be an example of the second. (Nothing will confirm your faith in the Fall like having to deal with car repairs!)

And if you are overexpecting, you will almost always be underexpecting in the same area. Remember, most underexpecters are really frustrated overexpecters.

When you jot down ways to be faithful in little, be specific. State your plans in terms you can review for progress. Ask your friend to help pray for and check up on you. Remember, a Christian friend or two is indispensable to the process. We succeed together or not at all.

Please be realistic even in the little things you choose to do. If you plan a number of changes, even though they are in little areas, it will be difficult to implement all of them at once.

Change comes in our Christian life not simply by knowing and understanding the truth, but by practicing it. James says we are to be doers of the word and not hearers only (see James 1:22-25). Therefore the remainder of this chapter, the part you will write, will be the most important yet. May God give you wisdom to balance your expectations biblically. And may His grace sustain you to be faithful in little.

## SAMPLE EXPECTATION CHART

Area of expectations _____

Pertinent Bible passages _____

What is expecting too much? _____

What is expecting too little? _____

How can I be faithful in little? (List specific steps and projected dates of implementation.) _____

_____

Explanation: Using the above sample as a guide, develop an expectation chart to help balance your own expectations. You might want to use a looseleaf notebook, with each page occupying a different expectation.

Topics you might want to deal with could include your job goals, marriage, children, singleness, education, housing, Bible study, prayer, social and political involvement, evangelism, discipleship, physical fitness, personal finances (including giving, saving, and debt reduction), fellowship and ministry in the church, and personal meditation and worship.

Begin with only a few areas. Be sure to include the one or two where you seem most frustrated.

Review your charts periodically to check progress and possibly adjust your expectations. Make your expectations a matter of prayer. Remember it is "God who brings the increase."

Stick with the exercises long enough to make balancing expectations a regular habit for you. Then you may no longer need to keep formal charts. The important thing is that you keep dealing with your expectations. They are, after all, the content of your faith and will help or hinder your growth in Christ.

## SOME EXAMPLES

Remember some of the frustrated baby boomers I described in earlier chapters of this book? Let's consider how they used the process I described above.

Jack and Susan used the expectation chart to help resolve their unfulfilled dreams of a house. After examining biblical passages on houses and contentment, they decided their expectations were too high. The Brady Bunch's house was much more than what they really needed and was not practical with their projected income.

Jack and Susan also decided that a home should be adequate for their family size, give opportunity for individual creativity and expression, not unduly strap them financially, and be a sound investment.

Their solution was to set aside extra money each month—after their giving and regular expenses—to be applied to future home improvement. Their idea was to do the best with what they have, adding special touches to the decor and livability of their present house without going heavily in debt.

Cathy, the depressed mother of preschoolers, worked on her expectation chart with her husband, Ron. Cathy decided that a perfect house, perfectly behaved children, and uninterrupted personal attractiveness were all overexpectations.

She is now trying to define more realistic standards for a clean house and growing children. Ron is helping out by providing an allowance for weekly house-cleaning help and a mother's day out. Cathy decided she can look really nice for at least a few hours each day and has arranged the children's naps so that she can leisurely bathe and dress just prior to Ron's arrival from work.

Cathy and Ron have proposed to review their expectations after six weeks and make modifications as necessary. Cathy has joined a support group at her church for mothers of preschoolers. She hopes this group will also help her keep her expectations in balance.

Jim, the workaholic dentist, decided his economic expectations are totally out of line with the financial realities of the eighties and nineties. Thus Jim has decided to give up his unrealistic dream of affluence and begin to enjoy the process of the life God has granted.

Jim is cutting back his office hours from sixty-plus to not more than forty-five per week. He will also sell his boat, one of his cars, and his membership at the country club.

He will retain his cabin in the mountains since it is paid for and will provide good family time free from distractions. Jim is also planning to increase both his giving and his involvement in his local church.

Both Frank, who was addicted to pornography, and Meg, who was addicted to shopping, saw a biblical counselor to help with their problems. Each found that their addictions were caused in part by unrealized expectations.

For Frank his habit helped him forget his unrealized career goals. Meg's overspending represented an attempt to get the attention of a noncommunicative husband and to ease the pain of her lone-liness in marriage.

Frank and Meg were counseled to set goals for being faithful in little in their areas of frustration. To start helping his career, Frank is now enrolled in a night class at a local junior college. Meg is reading a book on communication and working with her counselor to improve her marriage. Both Frank and Meg have established a system of accountability to help break their habits.

Sam, the frustrated pastor, saw the error of his quantitative view of success. After asking both God and his church to forgive him, Sam is trying to become more of a servant to his flock.

"I'm getting back to the basics," said Sam. "I'm going to do my best to love my people and proclaim God's Word regardless of the short-term numerical consequences. I'll serve the few or the many. The increase is up to God."

By the way, six months after Sam's new commitment, there has been a significant increase in the size of his congregation. Gary and Barb are typical of the new families who are now joining Sam's church.

"We always wanted a smaller church," explains Barb, "where the atmosphere is more personal and informal. But most small churches are so uptight over their smallness, they get pushy and overly demanding of their visitors. Pastor Sam and his people are not that way. We feel loved and accepted for who we are, not for what we might contribute. It's funny, but now we want to help all we can."

Sam learned that adjusting one's expectations in a fallen world is not as laborious as it sounded. It is the only wise thing to do and, in the long run, it is the least demanding on us, for overex-pecting only leads us to be frustrated and bitter. Perhaps this is what Jesus meant when He said, "My yoke is easy, and My load is light" (Matt. 11:30). If the yoke we are carrying seems too heavy, perhaps it is not the yoke He intended. Perhaps it is a self-imposed burden.

The Lord made us to serve Him with gratitude and, yes, joy. In the midst of a perverse world we can still laugh, sing, and generally enjoy life to the glory of God, but not when we are burdened with a self-imposed load of guilt and resentment.

# CHAPTER

# 8

## Baby Boomers in the Pew: How the Church Should Respond to Baby Boomers

How should the church respond to the baby boom? What should church leaders be, do, and teach in light of this generation that is now molding our culture?

First of all, there are two mistakes that must be avoided. One, we cannot simply ignore the baby boom; and two, we dare not conform to it.

The baby boom is simply too big and too influential to be ignored. Industries have been made or broken by the baby boom. Businesses have learned the hard way that you neglect the baby boom at your own peril.

A good example of the phenomenon is the Coca-Cola fiasco of 1985. In the spring of that year, Coke announced its decision to change the original Coke to a new, sweeter, less fizzy formula. Tests showed that teenagers liked the new Coke better, and teens drink more soft drinks than people in their twenties and thirties.

What Coke failed to remember is that the baby *bust* generation (today's teens) is relatively small. The much larger baby boom generation still controls the American market. Up to fifteen hundred phone callers a day brought back "Classic Coke," which, within a year's time, was outselling new Coke by four to one.[1]

Churches should learn a lesson from Coca-Cola. If we want to minister to today's society, we must speak to baby boomers in ways and words they can both accept and understand. We must be willing to "become all things to all men"—in this case, all 76 million of them.

Churches that ignore baby boom trends and insist on hanging on to traditional ways of doing things simply for the sake of tradition will find their ranks depleted by the end of the twentieth century. And in saying this, I am not just concerned about church attendance figures. If the people aren't attending church, it may mean the gospel isn't reaching them.

On the other hand, we dare not conform to baby boom ideology when it conflicts with biblical absolutes. If we do, we may win their hearts but lose their souls. The gospel that sells to this generation may not be the gospel that will save it. And make no mistake, this generation needs saving.

The following words sound like they would have appeared in a Christian periodical like *Moody Monthly*. They did not. They were part of an editorial in *Texas Business*.

We are truly the lost generation, huffing and puffing down the fast track to nowhere, always looking to the dollar sign for direction. That's the only standard we recognize. We have no built-in beliefs, no ethical boundaries. Cheat on your taxes, just don't get caught. Cheat on your wife, just don't get AIDS. Simply use a condom.

"Where did I go wrong?" is the traditional wail of parents of kids-gone-wrong. The eighties version says, "We gave him everything—clothes, a computer, a car, a college education." Everything but a conscience. We are products of a high-tech society: amoral automatons outfitted with calculating brains and sleek casings, just like the computers with which we are so compatible.

But they forgot to give us souls.[2]

These are the words not of some zealous fundamentalist preacher but of *Texas Business* editor-in-chief Brux Austin. Austin is decrying the recent scandals on Wall Street caused in part by "blindly ambitious baby boomers." Austin says that we have been programmed to acquire at the expense of both our personal integrity and our personal fulfillment.

> What good is lolling in your Jacuzzi in the beautiful backyard of your breathtaking home if you feel an aching emptiness in your innards—a chronic pain that all the wine cooler in the world can't numb?[3]

We cannot ignore the baby boom, and we dare not conform to its unbiblical ideology; but we must minister to it. The need is great. That ministry, however, will need to pass at least four tests in order to be effective.

## THE TEST OF UNDERSTANDING

If you decide to be a missionary to China, you need to be able to do more than understand the Chinese language well enough to speak it. You must also be able to understand Chinese culture and mentality well enough to think it. Otherwise you may use the same words but with conflicting meanings.

Church leaders, especially those raised in another generation and in a somewhat isolated Christian subculture, have often not understood the mind-set of the baby boom. Labeling us rebellious, self-centered yuppies may produce understanding nods from the already-convinced. It will not help reach the baby boom.

Rather, the church must address things like the epistemological gap between generations. It will not help to shout "Thus saith the Lord!" with grave certainty—not when baby boomers believe that what is truth for you may not be truth for them. Baby boomers need to be shown the absurdity of denying classical logic. They need to see the weakness in testing truth by experience alone. They need to see where their epistemology must ultimately lead them.

And the church must understand and address the overexpecter. Christian books and sermons directed to the underexpecter (there were plenty of those in earlier generations) will only increase the frustration of the baby boomers. We already expect too much.

The church must also understand and prepare for demographic changes brought on by the baby boom. Only 15 percent of today's families fit the model of the traditional nuclear family of the sixties. Seventy percent of mothers with young children now work outside the home. By 1990, 45 percent of all households will be headed by a single adult. Partly because of the escalating cost for raising children, one-fourth of this generation's parents will have only one child. Another one-fourth of the boom's married couples will have no children at all; the fertility rate of American women hit an all-time low in 1986.

What do all these statistics mean? They mean that church ministries designed for the needs of the sixties will not work in the eighties and nineties. While the church's message should never change, her methods must do so frequently. We must deal with society as it is, not as we hoped it might be.

Thus women's Bible studies that meet only on weekdays will miss most baby boom women. Family life conferences and couple's retreats will not speak to the single person. Christian camping will have fewer prospective children for resident camps, but day camps, like the day-care industry, will boom. Christian colleges (most of them, like most private colleges, having almost unbearably high tuition) will have fewer students available for resident education, but there will continue to be a large number of baby boomers interested in correspondence and extension courses.

*Understanding Negative Trends.* In order to minister to people where they are, we must adapt ministries to baby boom trends. However, at the same time, some of these trends must be firmly resisted in the church. Single parenting, for instance, is very much with us, but it is certainly not the best way to raise kids. Children need both parents, and the church must urge parents to stay together.

Of the growing number of single-parent households (now 7 million strong), the great majority (nine out of ten) are headed by a female.[4] Thus more and more children are being raised without a father. In fact, over half of these kids see their father less than once a month, including 31 percent who never see their father at all.[5] Yet according to Marilyn Elias, writing in *American Health,* "New research shows the ability to be a good buddy comes, for sons especially, from a close bond with Dad."[6]

Elias cites a study done at Loyola University in Chicago by psychologist Susan Kromelow. Kromelow tested the affects of parents on the social development of toddlers. Her tests led her to speculate that because dads tend to be more playful and "rough and tumble" with kids, they encourage more risk-taking.

Elias concludes: "Kromelow's study, though small, adds to a growing pool of new evidence that dads aren't minor props in the family drama, but play a vital role in their children's lives."[7] Thus secular research again verifies common sense and the biblical norm. Scripture portrays the fatherless as especially vulnerable and in need of extra protection.

Again, we must be realistic. Some single mothers must of necessity continue in their singleness as the best of two nonideal choices in a fallen world. The fathers of these children could be dead or remarried. Or the alternative could be physically abusive or unfaithful fathers who could be worse than no father at all. In this case the church should be ready to help out with volunteer pals for fatherless children, especially young boys.

Given the large number of working moms among the boom

women, day care for young children is another trend which seems to be here to stay. Seventy percent of baby boom women now work outside the home. Of those who have children, nearly half are back at work by their child's first birthday. "Among women with preschoolers, only one-third worked in 1970; the share today is 54 percent."[8] Thus Kinder Care, the largest operation of day-care centers in the U.S., projects an earnings growth of 35 percent annually for the next several years. But as Dr. Paul Meier and Linda Burnett have pointed out in their book *The Unwanted Generation*, day care can be hazardous to your child's physical and emotional health. The authors list and document ten very convincing reasons—things like increased susceptibility to communicable diseases, difficulty in forming strong personal relationships, and loss of identity and individualism, reasons which lead these authorities to believe that parents themselves furnish the best day care for their own children.[9]

But ideal home care may not be possible. Single mothers may have to work outside the home. Others may be forced by economic considerations to do the same. For instance, 69 percent of couples buying their first home in 1985 needed two incomes to afford the mortgage.[10] In such cases creative alternatives might be explored, especially for children not yet school age. Dr. Meier estimates that 85 percent of a child's personality development occurs by age six. Thus intense parental involvement is especially important during the preschool years.

So husbands and wives may be able to arrange work schedules so their children will spend a minimal number of hours in day care. Others may find willing relatives or friends. In such cases parents should be sure that this alternative is really better than day care. Neglect and abuse are not unique to professional sitters.

The church can help by providing support groups for homebound mothers, especially those with young children. This society will certainly not compliment them on their decision to sacrifice career for motherhood. It is, however, a high and lofty calling, and they need our encouragement. If women do not hear from the church that motherhood without a paying profession is a noble vocation in itself, they probably will not hear it elsewhere.

Economists now estimate that raising a child to age eighteen will cost between $150,000 and $200,000. Thus smaller families are the definite trend of this generation. But at least one Christian writer feels this too is a trend to be resisted. According to Harold O. J. Brown, a smaller population, especially of Christians, may not help our nation — not spiritually, not even economically. Fewer people, for instance, will not mean more job openings. "A shrinking population does not prevent unemployment; it creates new problems more difficult to handle."[11]

Ben Wattenberg of the American Enterprise Institute enumerates some of these problems. Speaking of the present "birth dearth" and its potential destabilizing effect on our society, Wattenberg warns: "I see the housing industry tearing its hair out. I see problems in the military. I see enormous problems headed this way with Social Security and retirement."[12]

In a *Christianity Today* article, Dr. Brown says that baby boom parents are producing less than the 2.1 children per family necessary for the present adult population to simply reproduce itself. He calls the phenomenon "the strangest collective suicide in history" and urges Christian couples to once again consider the command of Genesis 1:28 to "be fruitful and multiply."

> Multiplying Christians could only be salutary for society. And for once Christians could set a good trend, instead of complaining about bad ones.[13]

C. S. Lewis probably would have agreed with Dr. Brown. Lewis wrote, "As long as Christians have children and non-Christians do not, one need have no anxiety for the next century."[14]

Again, having more children may not be possible for some. In fact, Dr. Brown points out that over 50 percent of American families no longer have a choice in the matter since one or both partners are sterile.

Others may have other good reasons for having few or no children. But some should probably reconsider. Child-rearing is a tough job, but according to God it is a significant and blessed one.

> Behold children are a gift of the LORD;
> The fruit of the womb is a reward.
> Like arrows in the hand of a warrior,
> So are the children of one's youth.
> How blessed is the man whose quiver
>     is full of them
> (Ps. 127:3-5).

And while there are valid reasons for choosing singleness or childlessness in our day, there is also an invalid reason.

Many baby boomers who choose singleness or childlessness in our day are doing so because of blatant narcissism. "Why get married?" asks Ken, a typical baby boom bachelor. "Haven't you noticed? Single men of my age are in demand. I can have many women for friends and lovers and never have to support any of them."

Consider the case of Steve and April, who are what one publication calls DINKS (Double Income couples with No Kids). "Why have children?" asks Steve. "Neither April nor I particularly like kids, and if we had them, think of all we would have to give up—leisurely nights alone, frequent meals out, new cars, vacations abroad."

Now, neither singleness nor childlessness is inherently bad. In fact, the apostle Paul preferred the single state to being married. However, his reason for doing so is drastically opposed to the narcissism of the baby boom.

But I want you to be free from concern. One who is unmarried is concerned about the things of the Lord, how he may please the Lord; but one who is married is concerned about the things of the world, how he may please his wife, and his interests are divided. And the woman who is unmarried, and the virgin, is concerned about the things of the Lord, that she may be holy both in body and spirit; but one who is married is concerned about the things of the world, how she may please her husband. And this I say for your own benefit; not to put a restraint upon you, but to promote what is seemly, and to secure undistracted devotion to the Lord (1 Cor. 7:32-35).

Paul says married people have legitimate distractions in their families that limit their service to God. Single people do not. Thus they have more time and energy — not to pamper themselves, but to serve God by selflessly serving others. Thus your singleness or childlessness should not free you to serve yourself more, but others.

Baby boomers avoiding marriage or children because of selfishness need to remember the advice of King Solomon.

Where no oxen are, the manger is clean,
but much increase comes by the strength of the ox
(Prov. 14:4).

Narcissistic lives may be very uncluttered. In God's sight they are also very unproductive. Oxen make for messy mangers. They also make for productive fields. You have a God-given right to choose singleness or childlessness. You do not have a right to choose selfishness. In God's book there can be no success without service.

The irony of it all is that in the long run, the childbearing baby boomers may have proved to have served themselves well by serving their children, as demographer Cheryl Russell points out.

> Even in a modern, wealthy society, and despite the enormous Social Security system, the elderly need children as insurance for a happy and healthy old age. The millions of baby boomers who consider remaining childless do not realize that the most important long-term investment they can make is to have children. It's not the childless who are selfish. It's the people who have children who are selfishly—and wisely—guarding their old age.[15]

By the way, do not be fooled by the current baby boomlet, the term given to the large number of babies being born in the mideighties. The phenomenon is due to the fact that the ranks of women in the childbearing years are now filled almost entirely by baby boomers. There are more potential mothers available, but the *percentage* of women having babies is not increasing. Births will drop drastically in the nineties as baby boom mothers are replaced with women of the baby bust generation.

Please notice that all of these examples of negative baby boom trends have dealt with the family. Increasing divorce rates, day care, and fewer or no children—these all challenge the biblical concept of the family. There is a reason for citing these trends in particular. The baby boom has been harder on the family than any previous generation in American history. Landon Jones concurs:

> In the space of a decade, the boom generation had demolished many of our oldest ideas about marriage and family. In doing so, it had come close to balkanizing the institution of the family itself. It had broken down many of the links between husbands and wives, between parents and

children, between grandchildren and grandparents. Parenthood had been devalued. America was no longer a society dominated by children or even by families. As families continued to break down, more and more children were caught up in divorce and grew up with a different idea — if any idea at all — of how the traditional family operated.[16]

So many, if not most, of the baby boom trends to resist will come in the area of family. The church today must help save and restore families.

And in order to resist these negative trends concerning the family, we will need to first change our expectations. Let me illustrate with the most tragic baby boom trend to date — abortion on demand.

Father James Burtchaell of the University of Notre Dame sees a definite link between the prochoice position and overexpectations. Citing a recent study of activists on both sides of the issue Burtchaell writes,

> Prochoice activists expected life not to deal them an unjust hand, and that they must not be expected to carry unwanted burdens too long. The prolife activists, in contrast, understood some hardship as written into the script of life. They saw suffering as something we have no right to expect to avoid or evade by choice.[17]

Thus, according to Father Burtchaell we will not totally solve the abortion problem by recriminalizing the practice (that is, getting a reversal on the landmark 1973 Supreme Court decision that, in effect, decriminalized most abortions). While such a reversal should be aggressively pursued, Burtchaell believes it will still not prevent a large number of abortions. These will only cease when we return to more biblical expectations.

The prochoice movement has echoed the unfortunate priority of our culture: that one always has a right to freedom of choice. The Christian tradition, which fastens its attention more on needs than on choice, finds it amusing that anyone should identify freedom of choice with parenting. What could be a worse warrant for child-rearing than an insistence on getting just what you want? What could set you up for a bigger fall than to expect your child to satisfy your roster of hopes? Children exist to destroy hopes — and then to replace them with enhanced hopes.[18]

So the church must help parents return to more biblical expectations of parenthood. You don't have a child for the same reason you buy a pet. We do not raise them primarily for our pleasure. To be sure, there are joys in child-rearing, but these are often the exception rather than the rule, especially in the short run. To view it any other way is to invite disillusionment of parents and victimization of children. Both prochoice and prolife advocates know that child-rearing is often a painful vocation, but prolife people are realistic enough to know that, in the long run, the world benefits from loving parents that rear their children with great care.

*Understanding Positive Trends.* Not all baby boom trends need to be resisted. Some are positive and need our encouragement. To understand the baby boom, church leaders must also understand its strengths, and there are many.

Baby boomers have a high regard for genuineness, in themselves and in others. They readily admit failure. They are not often hypocritical.

Similarly, their intellectual honesty is challenging. They are not afraid to ask tough questions. Their high degree of education has given them quick minds that, when regenerate, are capable of an unusual mastery of biblical truth.

Their innovation and freedom from traditionalism can be refreshing. Their openness and vulnerability make fellowship real and particularly edifying. Older church people, watching innovations in church practice, often say, "We never did it that way before." In many cases (as every pastor knows too well), this is tradition for tradition's sake, and no other reason exists. Most baby boomers are not afraid of trying something new in worship or Sunday school. Whatever their other failings are, boomers are seldom guilty of being tradition-bound.

Even their arrogance is often admirable. Baby boomers have never been satisfied with the status quo, and if we can only learn that change often comes slowly and with a great deal of prayer and work, we will attempt great things for both man and God. So Christian baby boomers with balanced expectations will not be intimidated by the seemingly insurmountable problems of the 1990s. It will not matter that others have failed. Rather, like those optimistic realists of the first-century church, we will seek to turn our world upside down for Jesus Christ.

So smart church workers will capitalize on the strengths of their baby boomers. They will provide opportunity for smaller sharing and caring groups where real fellowship can be maximized. They will encourage intensive Bible study in a setting where tough questions are not dodged. They will provide fresh, innovative, yet thoroughly biblical worship experiences. And they will take on challenging projects as a group.

Thus the church, especially its leadership, must understand the baby boom. We need a crash course in baby boom culture. Such will not be difficult. There is an abundance of material available. Landon Jones' *Great Expectations* would be a good place to start reading. After that, there are a number of articles appearing frequently in the major periodicals. And many popular films, such as the 1987 comedy *Baby Boom* offer insights into the baby boom mentality.

As this book goes to press, there are a number of new trends appearing, due mostly to the aging of the baby boom. For instance, as the baby boom ages there is a definite trend away from single-ness and back to marriage, away from mobile marrieds and back to family, children, and staying at home ("couch potatoes"), away from the blatant yuppie greed of the mid-eighties and back to the more other-centered values of the sixties, away from materialism and back to an increased interest in spiritual things, evidenced by an increase in church attendance. Again, wise church leaders will be aware of these trends and capitalize on them for the sake of the gospel.

## THE TEST OF VULNERABILITY

If you are going to be a leader of baby boomers in business, poli-tics, or the church, you must be authentic, realistic, and vul-nerable.

Why was Richard Nixon attacked so mercilessly by the baby boom press? What was his unforgivable sin? For this generation, the sin of hypocrisy heads our most hideous sin list. We will under-stand and empathize with one who fails, but not with one who fails and covers up.

Perhaps the lack of vulnerability among so many of our leaders is what has made the baby boom claim so few heroes. When the Princeton class of 1969 was asked ten years later whom they most admired, the leading choice was "Nobody." [19]

We need more church leaders like C. S. Lewis, that prolific Brit-ish author and Christian apologist who never tried to conceal his humanity. His statement in *The Problem of Pain* is a good ex-ample. In this still popular classic on the subject of suffering, Lewis writes,

> You would like to know how I behave when I am experienc-ing pain, not writing books about it. You need not guess, for I will tell you; I am a great coward. [20]

Baby boomers relate to statements like that. Our shattered expectations have made us realists. We listen to people who are vulnerable. Tina Turner sang the song "We Don't Need Another Hero." But in fact, everyone, baby boomers included, do need heroes, though for them the heroes must be real, and being real includes being vulnerable.

But vulnerability is not always so easy. It brings risks. People who cannot handle their own humanity may not be able to handle ours either.

Biblical writers took that risk and, as a result, we find great encouragement in their lives. The same David who slew Goliath also struggled with fear. The same Peter who denied the Lord faced His executioners on Pentecost. The great apostle who took the gospel to Europe struggled intensely with his own fallenness. Because they were candid about their humanity, we find hope for us too. If God used them, He can use us.

## THE TEST OF BIBLICAL TEACHING

More than anything else, this generation needs biblical teaching. Our minds need to be renewed with expectations born not in the culture, but in the Word of God.

We need to teach biblical epistemology. Baby boomers need to know that all truth is not relative, and experience is only one test of truth—often misleading in the short run.

Indications are that our greatest threat in the waning years of the twentieth century will not be secular humanism but false religious mysticism. The success of authors like Shirley MacLaine illustrate the point. Baby boomers are turning to faith, but not the faith of our fathers. They are finding their God not in the Scriptures but in themselves. Our greatest threat in public education is coming not from teachers who peddle rationalistic evolution but from those who promote irrational psychotechnologies.

And, as Dave Hunt has pointed out, the church has not been unaffected. There has been "a seduction of Christianity," the title of a book he coauthored.[21] Many Christians have bought the false mysticism of the New Age movement.

Hunt has recently come under much criticism for his words.[22] Some accuse him of overstating his case. (For instance, he tends to discount all psychology and psychologists as humanistic.)[23] Others don't like his guilt-by-association techniques. (He quotes James Dobson as an example of those who promote a false doctrine of self-esteem.[24])

But we must not be guilty of the same error of which we accuse Hunt. Hunt has been accused of throwing out the proverbial baby with the bath water. We dare not do the same. You see, Hunt's basic thesis is both well-documented and true to reality. When Old Testament Israel fell into idolatry, it did not always expel the worship of the true God. Rather, like King Ahaz, the Hebrews often set up their pagan deities alongside the other furniture in the temple of the true God.

Dave Hunt is right. Twentieth-century Christendom is in danger of the same kind of idolatry. "Christian" meditation techniques are sounding more like the spiritist's astral travel than the biblical ponderings of the ancient Hebrew psalmist. Prayer has, for some Christians, become more like a witch doctor's spell than the apostle's petition.

Rather than confessing Jesus as Lord, baby boomers are confessing themselves as godlike. Shirley MacLaine says that one of the greatest discoveries any individual can make is that he himself is God. And all that will save us from this and similar errors is a return to biblical epistemology. When truth is absolute and the Scripture is our authority, we can tell the idols from the elements of true Christianity. Consider these words by Chuck Colson.

Christianity rests on the belief that God is the source of truth and that he does not alter it according to the spirit of the times. When Christians sever their ties to absolute truth, relativism reigns, and the church becomes merely a religious adaptation of the culture.[25]

On the other hand, while drawing lines between Christian teaching and non-Christian teaching, we also need to acknowledge that all truth is indeed God's truth. Many baby boom believers enjoy secular books, films, and plays. This can be a good thing, so long as they can learn to separate valid insights from attitudes that are actually opposed to the Word of God. Few baby boomers will follow the lead of many older Christians who culturally isolate themselves from the secular world. Baby boomers are a relatively sophisticated bunch in regard to music, art, and film. While we would do well to steer them away from the more questionable forms of popular culture (pornography in its various forms, for example), we can let them know that the church has little to fear from the best in art and literature. The church should, without sacrificing its biblical truth, show that it is not opposed to culture in general. Exhibiting a negative attitude toward art and literature will only alienate baby boomers who enjoy intellectual and aesthetic stimulation.

We also need to show that we are not opposed to clear thinking. To use terms popularized by Francis Schaeffer, we need to teach baby boomers the difference between being *rational* and being *rationalistic*. Being rationalistic means beginning from a presupposition of atheism. Rationalistic people deny God and His Word. They live in a "closed" universe. They deny the very possibility of the supernatural. "The fool has said in his heart, 'There is no God' " (Ps. 14:1). The Bible says such thinking is foolish and wrong.

But being rational means only to think as God has made us, as He Himself is and thinks, to think in harmony with the law of contradiction. "A" cannot equal "non-A." We should encourage such thinking. Thus teachings that contradict Scripture are in error and must be exposed and rejected.

People like Anne, the psychic who holds to both Christianity and elements of the occult, need to be confronted. June, who says she loves Jesus, but at the same denies His deity, must be made aware of her inconsistency.

We need Sunday school classes on biblical hermeneutics. We need to learn to "rightly divide the Word of Truth" and proclaim again "the whole counsel of God." Our flocks must learn not only to proclaim but "contend for the faith."

The sins of one generation are not always the sins of the other, and Martin Luther once said that if we resist the spirit of the world in every area except the one it takes in our day, we fail to resist the world at all. In other words, avoiding the errors of past generations doesn't count for much if we end up looking like chameleons who adapt to our own society. Thus, we need to be tough on narcissism, isolationism, and regression and promote things like meekness, serving others, and winning together.

And we need a good shot of biblical realism. We need to teach biblical not cultural expectations. One good way to do this is to mix studies of doctrinal passages with narratives of biblical characters. Good character studies show us how to realistically mix theory with practice.

Studying the lives of the men and women of Scripture will also help us address the real issues in our day. To hear some modern-day sermons, you would think that the most serious problem faced by the average parishioner is a missed quiet time or two.

But the Bible addresses tough subjects like adultery, anger, drunkenness, prejudice, fear, sexual abuse, rebellious children, gray areas of decision making, homosexuality, and incest. And most of these struggles are seen in the context of the godly home, in the assembly of God's own. God's own were not immune to the real problems of their day. There were no ideal people, nor were there ideal homes.

Jerry and Darlene desperately need some answers. Two years ago their ideal Christian family was shattered by the discovery that their oldest son, Jeff, was addicted to cocaine. "Where did we go wrong," Jerry agonizes. "We did all the right things—home schooling, Christian schools, reading all the right books, attending all the seminars. And now Jeff just isn't my Jeff anymore."

The news stunned their church. Jerry and Darlene were good parents who genuinely loved their three boys and were seeking to train them biblically both in church and at home. Jeff was a quiet boy, but he never seemed particularly rebellious.

Now Jeff has been placed in a juvenile detention center after a conviction for felony theft. Jerry has resigned as a deacon in his church because, as he puts it, "I don't have my own house in order." He and Darlene feel they have failed, but they don't know where. And they don't know what to do now. "We must do something," says Darlene, "both for Jeff's sake and the other boys. There must be some answers."

Jerry and Darlene are not the first believers to agonize over family problems. King David was a man after God's own heart. His home, however, was a disaster. The story reads like a modern soap. David's first-born son, Amnon, raped his stepsister, Tamar. Tamar was later avenged by Absalom, another of David's sons, who in turn murdered his stepbrother Amnon. Absalom then led an insurrection against his own father and was himself killed.

King Hezekiah was one of the godliest of Judah's kings, yet his father, Ahaz, was an idolater. On the other hand, Hezekiah's own son, Manasseh, was as wicked as Hezekiah was righteous.

Such reality is certainly not anything to brag about. It is not good, but it did happen in biblical days, and it occurs all too frequently in our own day. And real problems will not go away by just burying our heads in the sand and pretending they are not here. Real problems must be addressed realistically from the Scriptures. The Bible was not written for perfect people living under perfect conditions. It was written for us.

## THE TEST OF COMPASSION

I was riding in the car one day recently listening to some good baby boom nostalgia music when John Denver's, "Annie's Song," came on. It's one of my favorites. The songs begins with a beautiful description of John's love for his bride, Annie. It's a love that filled up his senses. The song goes on to describe a love with commitment, a love that will last forever. John promises to give his life to Annie, to die in her arms, to always be with her.

The song ended, and a baby boom disc jockey, a girl in her late twenties, came on the air. Obviously choking back tears, she tried to announce the next selection.

I knew how she felt. You see, John and Annie are not together anymore. He won't always be with her. He didn't die in her arms. They split up, another baby boom dream shattered.

Like Elvis Presley and John Lennon, John Denver was a baby boomer hero. He was born in 1943 and is three years older than the oldest boomers. He is, however, one of the musical heroes of the baby boom. And his love and commitment to Annie were legendary. Theirs was the relationship we all dreamed of having.

Hearing "Annie's Song" that day made me think of another song popular with us baby boomers, a song made popular by Michael Martin Murphy. This was written by a man who obviously had such tragedies weighing heavily on him when he wrote:

> I've been looking at people
> And how they change with the times.
> And lately all I've been seeing are people
> Throwing love away and losing their minds.

Maybe it's me who's gone crazy.
But I can't understand why
All these lovers keep hurting each other
When good love is so hard to come by.

So what's the glory in living?
Doesn't anybody ever stay together anymore?
And if love never lasts forever,
Tell me, what's forever for?

And I see love-hungry people
Trying their best to survive,
When right there in their hands is a dying romance,
And they're not even trying to keep it alive.

So what's the glory in living?
Doesn't anybody ever stay together anymore?
And if love never lasts forever,
Tell me, what's forever for?[26]

If Rafe VanHoy's words don't move you, you've failed the test of compassion. Baby boomers may appear arrogant and self-centered. We also hurt deeply. Many of our dreams have died.

At first we wanted to make the world a better place. Then we just wanted to make our own corner of the world a better place, but neither worked. Reality shattered our dreams.

We've tried to handle our brokenness in a number of wrong ways—narcissism, regression, isolationism, cynicism. But the church will miss the point if it just harps on the sins of the baby boom. Many baby boomers, especially baby boom believers, already feel intense guilt. What we need is understanding, forgiveness, and hope. Pointing out our failings is a beginning, but it is not enough by itself.

Broken people need compassion. They also need a mender. They need the Savior. We need the one who promises to give hope to our brokenness, rest to our drivenness. We need Jesus.

And for the church today, her greatest test will come precisely at this point. In fact, all the other tests we've explored in this chapter lead to this one ultimate test. How well did we present Christ to the most decisive generation in the history of America? And what about those who do turn to Him? Will we be faithful in making disciples of baby boom believers?

# EPILOGUE

Much of this book has been devoted to exposing unrealistic and unbiblical expectations. Or to put it another way, I have tried to refute the happiness that is not, the gospel that is not, the modern teachings that are not in line with biblical expectations.

I did so, not just to tell the truth, though I believe that is a worthy goal in itself, but to help you discover the happiness that is, the true gospel. For you will never discover the true while still holding to the false.

The gospel of Jesus Christ really is good news. It is not a success gospel. It is a saving gospel. It will not free us from our struggle in this life. It will give us power to endure and grow over the long haul.

The gospel does not promise us riches or recognition in this life. It does guarantee us both in the one to come. It may not give us any of the things money can buy. It promises all of the things money cannot—real joy, peace, forgiveness, rest from our drivenness.

Simply put, it is a gospel worth believing.

# NOTES

CHAPTER 2

1. Landon Y. Jones, *Great Expectations: America and the Baby Boom Generation* (New York: Ballantine Books, 1980), 2.
2. Ibid., 42.
3. Ibid., 72.
4. Lee Atwater, quoted in *U.S. News and World Report*, 10 March 1986, 60.
5. *Fortune*, 5 August 1985, 74.
6. Jones, *Great Expectations*, 1.
7. Landon Y. Jones, "The Baby Boomers," *Money*, March 1983, 58.
8. Ibid., 300.
9. Ibid.
10. Ibid., 23.
11. Quoted in Jones, *Great Expectations*, 88.
12. Ibid., 53.
13. William Manchester, *The Glory and the Dream: A Narrative History of America, 1932-1972* (Boston: Little, Brown, and Co., 1974), quoted in Jones, *Great Expectations*, 53.
14. Ibid., 140.
15. Ibid., 140-141.
16. Jeff Greenfield, quoted in Jones, *Great Expectations*, 142.

CHAPTER 3

1. Arthur Anderson, quoted in *Forbes*, 29 August 1983, 166.
2. Ibid.
3. Ibid.
4. *Money*, March 1983, 57.
5. Ibid.
6. Ibid., 67.
7. *Newsweek*, 25 November 1985, 50.
8. *Forbes*, 29 August 1983, 166.
9. William Novak, *The Great American Man Shortage* (New York: Bantam Books, 1983).
10. Lee Ezell, *The Cinderella Syndrome* (Eugene, Oreg.: Harvest House Publishers, 1985), 40.
11. Ronald and Beverly Allen, *Liberated Traditionalism* (Portland, Oreg.: Multnomah Press, 1985), 39-40.
12. Jones, *Great Expectations*, 271.
13. Cheryl Russell, *One Hundred Predictions for the Baby Boom, The Next Fifty Years* (New York: Plenum Press, 1987), 120.
14. Ronald J. Vogel, quoted in the *Amarillo Globe Times*, 12 December 1983, 14.
15. *Newsweek*, 3 February 1986, 78.
16. Jones, *Great Expectations*, 299.
17. Ibid., 304.
18. Russell, *One Hundred Predictions*, 129.
19. Jones, *Great Expectations*, 296.
20. Ibid., 297-298.
21. *U.S. News and World Report*, 10 March 1986, 61.
22. *Psychology Today*, September 1987, 22.
23. *Newsweek*, 3 February 1986, 78.
24. Jones, *Great Expectations*, 306.
25. Ibid., 307.
26. *Newsweek*, 31 December 1984, 19.
27. *U.S. News and World Report*, 16 April 1984, 78.
28. *Newsweek*, 31 December 1984, 16.
29. *U.S. News and World Report*, 29 April 1985, 73.
30. *Newsweek*, 31 December 1984, 24.
31. Jim Meyers, "Sunset for Yuppies," *USA Today*, 13-15 November 1987, 1.
32. Ibid., 2.
33. Joanne Lipman, "Played Out: The Going Gets Tough and Madison Avenue Dumps the Yuppies," *The Wall Street Journal*, 9 December 1987, 16.

34. Quoted in Meyers, 2.
35. Ibid., 250.
36. Ibid.
37. Ibid., 242.
38. *Time*, 19 May 1986, 37.
39. Jones, *Great Expectations*, 254.
40. Ibid., 284.
41. Dan Kiley, *The Peter Pan Syndrome* (New York: Avon Books, 1983).
42. Jones, *Great Expectations*, 301.

CHAPTER 4

1. Francis Schaeffer, *Escape from Reason*, vol. 1 of *The Complete Works of Francis Schaeffer* (Westchester, Ill.: Crossway Books, 1982), 233.
2. Ibid.
3. Ibid., 229.
4. Ibid.
5. Allan Bloom, *The Closing of the American Mind* (New York: Simon and Schuster, 1987), 25-26.
6. Ibid.

CHAPTER 5

The teaching in this chapter is significant but not exhaustive truth. The identification principles in Romans 6 and the dynamics of the Spirit-led life in Romans 8 are balancing thoughts for this treatise. Please read and study them again to get the whole picture.

CHAPTER 6

1. *Newsweek*, 31 December 1984, 17.
2. Gordon MacDonald, *Ordering Your Private World* (Nashville, Tenn.: Thomas Nelson Publishers, 1984), 28-40.
3. Ibid., 33.
4. Ibid., 34.
5. Ibid., 32.
6. Ibid., 36.
7. Ibid., 33.
8. "Give Them All to Jesus." Written by Phil Johnson and Bob Benson. Copyright 1975 by Justin Time Music. All rights reserved. Used by permission of Gaither Copyright Management.

CHAPTER 7

1. C. S. Lewis, *God in the Dock*, ed. Walter Hooper (Grand Rapids, Mich.: William B. Eerdmans Publishing Co., 1970), 52.

CHAPTER 8

1. Russell, *One Hundred Predictions*, 49.
2. Brux Austin, *Texas Business*, June 1987, 5.
3. Ibid.
4. Russell, *One Hundred Predictions*, 105.
5. Ibid., 107.
6. Marilyn Elias, *American Health*, March 1987, 125.
7. Ibid.
8. Russell, *One Hundred Predictions*, 58.
9. Paul D. Meier and Linda Burnett, *The Unwanted Generation* (Grand Rapids, Mich.: Baker Book House, 1980), 47-62.
10. Russell, *One Hundred Predictions*, 55.
11. Harold O. J. Brown, "Not Enough Children," *Christianity Today*, 18 October 1985, 10.
12. John S. DeMott, "Welcome, America, to the Baby Bust," *Time*, 23 February 1987, 28.
13. Brown, "Not Enough Children."
14. Lewis, *God in the Dock*, 119.
15. Russell, *One Hundred Predictions*, 192-193.
16. Jones, *Great Expectations*, 254.
17. James T. Burtchaell, "In a Family Way," *Christianity Today*, 12 June 1987, 25.
18. Ibid., 27.
19. *Time*, 19 May 1986, 38.
20. C. S. Lewis, *The Problem of Pain* (New York: Macmillan Publishing Co., 1962), 105.
21. Dave Hunt and T. A. McMahon, *The Seduction of Christianity* (Eugene, Oreg.: Harvest House Publishers, 1985).
22. See Terry C. Muck, "Open Season," *Christianity Today*, 21 November 1986, 16-17.
23. Hunt and McMahon, *The Seduction of Christianity*, 189-191.
24. Ibid., 192-193.
25. Charles Colson, *Kingdoms in Conflict* (New York: William Morrow, 1987), 244.
26. Copyright 1978 Tree Publishing Co., Inc. International copyright secured. All rights reserved. Used by permission of the publisher.

## BOOKS AND ARTICLES ON THE BABY BOOM

Bloom, Allan. *The Closing of the American Mind.* New York: Simon and Schuster, 1987.

Burtchaell, James T. "In a Family Way." *Christianity Today,* 12 June 1987.

Byerly, Greg, and Richard E. Rubin. *The Baby Boom: A Selective Annotated Bibliography.* Lexington, Mass.: D. C. Heath and Co., 1985.

DeMott, John S. "Welcome, America, to the Baby Bust." *Time,* 23 February 1987.

Folkenberg, Judy. "Suicide: A Future Boom for Baby Boomers." *Psychology Today,* September 1987.

"Growing Pains at Forty." *Time,* 19 May 1986.

"Here Come the Yuppies." *Time,* 9 January 1984.

Huntley, Steve, with Gail Bronson and Kenneth Walsh. "Yumpies, YAP's, Yuppies—Who They Are." *U.S. News and World Report,* 16 April 1984.

Javna, John, and Gordon. '60s. New York: St. Martin's Press, 1983.

Jones, Landon Y. "The Baby Boomers." *Money,* March 1983.

———. *Great Expectations: America and the Baby Boom Generation.* New York: Ballantine Books, 1980.

Kaye, Tony. "The Birth Dearth." *The New Republic,* 19 January 1987.

La Bier, Douglas. "Life of a Yuppie Takes a Psychic Toll." *U.S. News and World Report,* 29 April 1984.

Lipman, Joanne. "Played Out: The Going Gets Tough and Madison Avenue Dumps the Yuppies." *The Wall Street Journal*, 9 December 1987.

Makower, Joel. *Boom! Talkin' about Our Generation*. Chicago: Contemporary Books, Inc., 1985.

Maloney, Lawrence D., with Michael Doan. "How Churches Try to Woo the Yuppies." *U.S. News and World Report*, 26 August 1985.

Moore, Thomas. "The New Libertarians Make Waves." *Fortune*, 20 July 1987.

O'Toole, Patricia. "Finding Work in Glutted Fields." *Money*, March 1983.

Rosellini, Lynn, with Stacy Wells. "When a Generation Turns Forty." *U.S. News and World Report*, 10 March 1986.

Runde, Robert. "Investing in the Boom." *Money*, March 1983.

Russell, Cheryl. *One Hundred Predictions for the Baby Boom, The Next Fifty Years*. New York: Plenum Press, 1987.

Samuelson, Robert J. "Selfishness and Sobriety." *Newsweek*, 8 April 1985.

———."Middle-aged America." *Newsweek*, 27 July 1987.

Smith, Lee. "The War between the Generations." *Fortune*, 5 August 1985.

Tuhy, Carrie. "What Price Children?" *Money*, March 1983.

Wallechinsky, David. *Midterm Report, The Class of '65: Chronicles of an American Generation*. New York: Viking Penguin, Inc., 1986.

Walsh, Kenneth T., with Gail Bronson, Jeannye Thoron, and Maureen Walsh. "The New-Collar Class." *U.S. News and World Report*, 16 September 1985.

"What Baby Boomers Make." *Newsweek*, 25 November 1985.

Will, George F. "Reality Says You Can't Have It All." *Newsweek*, 3 February 1986.

"The Year of the Yuppie." *Newsweek*, 31 December 1984.